CHANGES AMIDSHIPS

*The United States Naval Academy
1950s to 2020s*

The above photo, the photos on the front and rear covers and of the Chapel in Chapter 15 are courtesy of the USNA PhotoLab provided through the welcome assistance of Stacey Godfrey.

CHANGES AMIDSHIPS

*The United States Naval Academy
1950s to 2020s*

John Lynch, Class of 1960
and Robert Leam, Class of 2020

With Contributions from
Rick Bryant, Spencer McVeigh, and Joshua Haith,
Class of 2020

Jakobean Publishing Co.
Morristown, NJ

Copyright © 2021 by John F. Lynch, Jr. and Robert Leam
All Rights Reserved

Printed in the United States of America

*Dedicated to all who have had,
or will have,
the privilege of living part of their lives in
Bancroft Hall*

TABLE OF CONTENTS

Preface	ix
Acknowledgements and Choices	xiii
Introduction	1
Chapter One, Facilities	9
Chapter Two, Bancroft as a Facility	15
Chapter Three, Plebe Summer	21
Chapter Four, Daily Life in Bancroft, Then	31
Chapter Five, Academics, Then	37
Chapter Six, Academics, Now	47
Chapter Seven, Daily Life in Bancroft, Now	51
Chapter Eight, Youngster Cruise	61
Chapter Nine, Second Class Summer, Part I	69
Chapter Ten, Second Class Summer, Part II, Aviation	75
Chapter Eleven, Discipline, Demerits and Discharges	83
Chapter Twelve, King Hall	91
Chapter Thirteen, Liberty and Leave	99
Chapter Fourteen, Hazing	103
Chapter Fifteen, Pranks	109
Chapter Sixteen, Religion	119
Chapter Seventeen, Women	123
Chapter Eighteen, Race	135
Chapter Nineteen, First Class Summer	143
Chapter Twenty, Retention	149
Chapter Twenty-One, Wrapping Up	153
Epilogue	161
Appendix A	163
Appendix B	167

PREFACE

In early 2020 members of the United States Naval Academy class of 1960 were looking forward to a fall gathering for their 60th reunion. Then the nation went into its coronavirus lock down.

Back in Annapolis the campus was shuttered and the students dispersed to continue their studies by remote and socially distanced means at their families' homes or wherever else they could.

A 60th reunion was certainly a cause for reflection. As a member of that class who had been back to the campus roughly annually over the decades, my early 2020 reflections were balanced with questions about the changes that appeared to have occurred. Were they superficial? Unlikely. But how many of the details of our long ago daily lives still remained in the lives of our 60-year echo class? How much of the essence? And, by the way, what was the essence?

Could the old adage, "the more things change, the more they stay the same" be valid amid all the changes obvious at Navy?

Thoughts flowed from those questions. First, my classmates (and, likely, graduates from other classes around that time) were probably wondering the same things. Perhaps if I could get answers to my questions and write them up, that would help others answer their questions. Second, the best source for the answers I was looking for was likely a member of the about-to-graduate class of 2020. And members of that class were probably more accessible now that they were COVID-scattered and not as driven by Navy's relentless clock.

I hoped to find and interview a random but local Midshipman through the local high school or the local Catholic prep school. Both schools often send grads to Navy but neither was in a return-a-phone-call mode.

But the Naval Academy Alumni Association was, even though the return phone calls came from staff members working from their homes. They were eager to help. They gave me contacts around campus for current info and archived photos. But, most importantly, they put me in touch with an about-to-graduate senior who might answer my questions.

Within days I was talking to and quickly working at a level I had not expected with Robert Leam. Rob jumped in with an enthusiasm born of the belief that his class might wonder about the differences as well.

Rob and I are as markedly different as our Naval Academy experiences. I had entered school 5 weeks after my high school graduation as one of the youngest in my class; he had entered 5 years after he left high school, having had an extra year of schooling, done construction work, worked winters as a ski instructor, and then been in the fleet as an aviation mechanic rising to Petty Officer 3rd class. That difference had many effects. The most important of which, it seemed to me, was the difference in our relative maturity level at the time of our observations. We both had been reasonably successful academically. But he was much more successful than I at fitting in to the school's military culture—witness the fact that I had always marched in the ranks of my company, he had marched as a member of the Brigade staff at the head of the parade in what he called "the wedge."

Rob and I worked well together within our competencies. But when it came to addressing change in the matters of race and gender, we knew that our generally positive view of the current situation might not reflect the reality as seen by people more directly involved. So Rob set out to recruit friends among his classmates to be contributors on those issues. Those he asked and who agreed to serve were, for the African-American perspective, Rick

Bryant and Josh Haith (after graduation assigned to the Academy while awaiting fall classes at nuclear power and flight school, respectively) and, for the female perspective, Spencer McVeigh (who was headed for the surface Navy and an earlier-convening school for Surface Warfare Division Officers). They too, chipped in with enthusiasm both on their specific topics and with factual and other editorial input. Their pictures will come later.

We all had a reverence for the place. But we understood that primarily we were writing for our classmates. A consequence flowed from that. Our product was not intended to have a formality it might have had were we trying to convey our reverence to young men and women thinking about attending or to our common benefactors, the tax-paying public. We were not going to avoid salty language where it fit, though we would occasionally temper the language where it might unduly offend a more casual reader.

We hoped to remind our classmates of perhaps forgotten details that might trigger a memory and bring a smile. And we hoped that, if a wife (or a widow) read our version of days that had stayed in her memory as a time of young love, dress parades, and formal dances, she might whisper "Oh my!"

If either hope comes to be, we will have succeeded.

Lastly, we knew that others had written published books about our school and we had an obligation to our audience to not write some tedious repetition of those works. So we reviewed those that seemed most relevant.

There was Sweetman's *The United States Naval Academy: An Illustrated History*, 2nd (Cutler) edition. It is an impressive and glossy book that serves as a good source of facts. But, understandably, it reminded me of books from my Catholic high school years—Catholic books about the history of the Catholic Church: facts, yes, but overall clearly written by someone trying to say something nice about every pope. For Sweetman and Cutler, Superintendents were their popes. In fact, the signatures of eleven Superintendents appear at the front of the book where a Catholic history would bear an *imprimatur*. No doubt company history books commissioned by General Motors, IBM, or American Widget would have the same feel. Sweetman and Cutler wrote of the best of the school from a Superintendent's perspective; we hoped to write of the unvarnished but fondly remembered reality of the school from graduates' perspectives.

The title of a second book, Gelfand's *Sea Change at Annapolis: The United States Naval Academy, 1949-2000*, suggested some other grad may have trod our path before us. Not so. It is an insightful work of serious scholarship speaking to its readers about a conservative institution's adjustments to the liberalizing trend of the society it served. It reported on changes at Navy through the second half of the 20th century. Specifically, it examined changes regarding race (1949 marked the graduation of the first African-American from Navy), women (the first were admitted in 1976, by direction of Congress), and religion (compulsory chapel ended at the beginning of 1973 by direction of the Courts).

We also turned to two books by Vietnam combat veteran alums from the '60s, books we had already read, Navy Cross wearer Senator Jim Webb's *A Sense of Honor*, a novel set in Bancroft Hall, and Robert Timberg's *The Nightingale's Song*, a journalist's report on how the lives of 5 prominent Americans (from the classes of 1958, 1959, and 1966—including Webb) were shaped by their common experiences at Navy's seminary.

Such books provided details and corrected some faulty recollections. But fundamentally this work is different from the others. It is not as speak-no-evil reverential as Sweetman's, as scholarly sober as Gelfand's, nor as character-centered as Webb's or Timberg's. And we have chosen not to detail the glories of our athletically accomplished classmates as ours is a book of more universal experiences though their successes in their sports were both significant on the national stage and to our enjoyment of our time rooting them on. In like manner we have chosen not to name the characters whose deeds enrich our story. Ours is simply the product of our individual memories with all the limitations of accuracy, scope, and representative nature of tales told that individual memories involve. Yet it has its roots in the graduates' instincts set to song in the second stanza, the "alumni" stanza, of the Alma Mater, *Navy Blue and Gold*:

> Four years together by the Bay,
> Where Severn joins the tide,
> Then by the service called away,
> We're scattered far and wide,
> **But still when two or three shall meet**
> **And old tales be retold...**

That said, Rick, Spencer, Josh, Rob, and I truly hope you enjoy.

Very respectfully,

Jack

ACKNOWLEDGMENTS AND CHOICES

Acknowledgments

EVERY AUTHOR KNOWS THAT EVEN A BOOK FULL OF INDIVIDUAL recollections and personal opinions would never get into print without the willingness of others to support and assist the effort with open hearts. Rob and I have had the benefit of the go-out-of-their-way efforts of a whole host of folks and our work is the better for it.

That started with people at the Naval Academy Alumni Association when, hunkered down in their homes, they responded with the speed and courtesy that would have been extraordinary had we reached them in fully functioning offices with a demanding boss looking over their shoulders. They established our initial contact, gave us names and numbers of other normally-on-campus people who, in like manner, responded from their homes as the pandemic required. Thereafter they kept us on the right track whenever we sought their guidance. Particular among them we should mention Santina Rivera (the wife of an alum, Rick, of the Class of '94) and Holly Powers. It turned out that Holly was already involved in a task somewhat like ours. We kept comparing notes as our respective projects advanced which, at least from our side of the dialogue, was to our considerable and continuing advantage.

The folks from the Alumni Association also connected us to the staff at the Nimitz Library, most notably the Archivist, Dr. Jennifer Bryan. Dr. Bryan answered questions and pointed us to accessible collections that we would not have even thought about. She also honored our questions, even some which could not be answered, until she knew for sure the answers or that, after intervening decades, they could not be found even with considerable diligence.

Our experienced and incredibly diligent and meticulous editor, Kathleen Daley, has saved us from a boatload of errors and deserves our profound gratitude. Master Chief Michael Allen, USN, provided comments and additional edits, particularly on military form, which also enhanced the final product.

Classmates, schoolmates, and rivals supported our effort with wit and wisdom when we called on them, even out of the blue. Captain Jim McKinney, Captain David (Tug) Knorr, Glenn Coleman, Bob Meck, Rear Admiral Skip McGinley (USNA class of 1961), and LCOL. Bob Totten, USMA (class of 1960) are representative of those willing supporters.

This book contains almost 50 images. Some are personal photographs by the authors or of the authors taken by their friends. Most others are in the public domain obtained from Navy sources including the archives of the Nimitz Library at the Naval Academy (including from the archived class yearbooks of the classes of 1958 and 1960). We are grateful for the assistance we received from many in the service or otherwise employed by the Navy as we gathered these pictures and for the permission of the Office of the Navy Information allowing that assistance. For our use of these images the Navy requires that we state that, "Use of released U.S. Navy imagery does not constitute product or organizational endorsement of any kind by the U.S. Navy."

Above and beyond, support came from our contributors, friends and classmates whom Rob enlisted in this effort when humility required that we admit we were not the right people to give believable opinions on the state of affairs affecting categories of Midshipmen to which we did not belong. Rick Bryant shared his experience at the Academy as an African-American and Spencer McVeigh accepted a similar role as a woman. She had previously published about the topic in Annapolis' Capital Gazette (the excellent local newspaper with a tragic recent history) and was a perfect choice. Josh Haith joined on to cover the same beat as Rick but went on to contribute to many other sections, notably the Honor System where he had served as a member of the adjudicatory Brigade Honor Board.

Finally each of us personally owes a deep debt of gratitude to family and friends who supported our immersion in this project when their calls on our time were entitled to at least as much respect. As the only married person in our cabal, Jack's debt to his clearly better half, Doreen, for her forbearance and for her technical assistance is likely the deepest of all.

Style choices

As we wrote this book Rob and I decided we'd generally narrate the story from off-stage, describing things as facts not as personal observations though many of them are. Yet we do butt in from time to time identifying a personal observation or opinion. These interruptions appear as *Jack – blah, blah* or *Rob – something or other*.

In many places we present the comparison of our times at USNA with a full recitation of the earlier time followed by a similar description of the later period. In most cases these observations come one after the other in the same chapter. The one exception is the use of two separate and separated chapters when describing Daily Life in Bancroft Hall. At other times we use a more prompt comparative format with a 1960 fact followed in the next sentence, or sometimes in the same sentence, with a comparable 2020 fact—a more staccato comparison.

Some discussions are so opinion-laden that we abandon the offstage narrative and take personal responsibility for our statements.

We use 4/C, 3/C, 2/C, and 1/C consistently instead of multiple diverse other ways to identify the years known elsewhere as freshman, sophomore, etc. We trust that even an unfamiliar reader will quickly get the hang of these classes, these ranks, after a page or two just remembering that the higher the number the lower the status[1], just as it was with classes on the Titanic. With a similar trust we have chosen to use military time: 1600 for 4 o'clock in the afternoon, for example.

Though the class of 2020 has now graduated, in this book about what was and what is, it represents the now so we have knowingly used the present tense a bit more than is justified.

Also, in these days of a two-gender Academy we sometimes use "H/H" for "him or her" or "his or hers" or "H/S" for "he or she" (but never "they" for either singular alternative). When we use the likes of H/S often in a section we define it. But if a "he or she" shows up in isolation, we rarely use the abbreviation lest some reader have to pause to search H/H memory for what it means.

Lastly, where we thought it was worth referring you to the internet for further information, we have included both an easy-to-type link and a QR code (placed at the end of the relevant chapter). To follow the link, type the link address into your browser or point your mobile device's camera at the QR code.

We hope these choices make your time with our effort more enjoyable.

---

1 E.g., a 4/C is a freshman, a "plebe;" 3/C is a sophomore, a "youngster," etc., up to a 1/C is a soon-to-graduate senior.

INTRODUCTION

Change, but from what?

On Monday, June 25, 1956 USNA welcomed the class of 1960. On that day, as it had for 43 straight years, it swore in Mids to serve a nation of 48 states with 48 stars on its flag. It may not have seemed like it on that day at the venerable institution, but waves of change were lapping at its shores. When those Mids graduated 4 years later, they would be the first class sworn in to serve a nation of 50 states and the only class to be sworn in before a flag with 49 stars.

Those changes and much more important ones in the history of the institution were to come both during the time that the class of '60 was in "the Yard" and between then and now.

Probably most would agree that the biggest change has been in the demographics of the student body.

The 1,080 individuals admitted as the class of 1960 were all male, overwhelmingly Caucasian, and required to be "straight."

In June, 2016 the 1,184 entering members of the class of 2020 included 853 men, and 331 women (28%); their ranks included 399 students identified as minorities (34%). Neither the nation nor the school made any demands about their sexual orientation.

This book is about change at the Naval Academy over 64 years. For the Classes of 1960 and 2020 perceptions of such a time span must differ. For the members of 1960, 64 years is a fraction, about three quarters, of their lives; for the class of 2020 64 years is roughly three times the length of theirs.

Induction into the class of 1960

I-day, Class of 2020, with the plebe summer detail standing at the end of each row

We all have an understanding of what American society in 2020 is like. So, to convey a sense of time we'll start by reminding us all of America's changes over that span of time by mentioning what the class of 1960 understood of its time when it convened in 1956.

All members of the class of 1960 were born in the '30s. By the time most of them formed memories, their parents' generation was fighting WWII. Several members of the class lost fathers in that war, some before they really knew each other.

On the home front, private consumption deferred to the demands of the war both voluntarily and through government rationing. The only meats easily available because they were not rationed were organ meats such as liver and kidneys that the armed forces didn't serve the troops.

When members of the class of 1960 were born, for most of America outside the south, and with the exception of specific urban districts like Harlem, the African-American community was largely out of sight and out of mind. To a significant degree that changed during the war as many of its members went north to feel *The Warmth of Other Suns*[1] and find work in war industries. Even there, *de facto* segregation was so endemic that often the federal government had to step in, buy land, and build housing for those workers, thus strong-arming families into places where locals, left to their own devices, would not allow them. After the war, towns often spun off those neighborhoods. Towns like Victory Gardens, New Jersey remain scattered around the nation.

In those years a child's entertainment came from 10¢ comic books or radio shows. Most may not remember the names but can still identify in an instant the voice of Brace Beemer, the *Lone Ranger*, or Frank Readick, Jr., the narrator of *The Shadow*. Sports and games were a big part of their lives, but outside of school those sports were run by the kids as pick-up games. Rules like "into the maple is a do-over" or "over the fence is out" were consensual and highly local. For most in the class of 1960 parent-involved organized sports didn't exist; Little League didn't get to their towns until after they were too old to join. If in the earlier of those years a child had gone to the beach at the Jersey Shore, he would be cautioned to stay away from the "tar balls" (sticky softball-sized spheres of coagulated Bunker C fuel oil floating in from the ships sunk by U-Boats just off shore).

To lessen the U-boat risk, cars in coastal places had the top half of their headlights painted black. Meanwhile those cars and cars across America sat at the curb, often for the duration, because the sticker in their windshield limited the amount of gas their owners could buy.

Members of the class of '60's later childhood years were economically prosperous[2] for the nation, particularly compared to pre-war years. This was primarily due to two factors coming out of that war. First, industrial capacity had been war-elevated and producers were using it to meet the demands that had been deferred during the war and the related high level of household formation after the conflict. Second, the government policies of gratitude to those who served, reflected in the G.I. Bill, primed the pump through both educational assistance and support of home purchases and construction. That pump set off a tide that raised all boats. The United States, barely physically touched by the war, accounted for 50% of the

---

1. Isabel Wilkerson's 2010 history of "America's Great Migration."

2. Prosperity was not constant. The business cycle was afflicted by sharp, virtually triennial recessions.

world's industrial production.

One product of the war weighed heavily on '60's childhood: "atomic" weapons. Pictures of Hiroshima were in the press in 1945 and the Crossroads test of the effects of nuclear weapons on ships was radio-broadcast live from Bikini Atoll in the summer of 1946. At first the bomb was just a bodacious weapon. But in 1949 the Soviet Union ended America's monopoly on the bomb. By 1952, when the youngest members of the class of 1960 were entering high school, both nations had thermonuclear weapons. From then on the threat of a surprise attack by the Soviets was a matter of common public discussion. In grammar school classrooms across the country, children were taught to "Duck and Cover" when the seemingly inevitable flash of nuclear light occurred. People even outside tornado alley built and stocked underground shelters.

Even without war, above ground nuclear tests by America and the Soviets were spewing radioactive material, "fallout," across the globe. The calcium-like fission product, strontium-90, was falling on pastures and showing up in milk and children's bones. America's largest test, of an unintentionally large 15-megaton bomb (Hiroshima times 1000) happened in 1954. Even on the day the class of 1960 was sworn in, the United States exploded a 1.1 megaton device at Bikini Atoll.

But, to return to tangible details not fears, household electronics (apart from the radio) were non-existent. Even calculators, those transistor-enabled, wallet-sized conveniences most remember, now simply an app on a pocket phone, were typewriter-sized office machines. The transistor was a post-war invention at Bell Labs (a national treasure of pure science protected from quarterly results pressure by being within the AT&T monopoly).[3]

Back then phones were wired to the wall. They didn't have touch tone dialing (until 1963) and many didn't even have rotary dialing. Most '60 Mids who grew up outside an urban area (and it didn't matter whether from New England, the Ozarks, or the intermountain west), had experienced operator-assisted only local calls at some point, many had party lines. Even into the '60's "Pittsburgh 19, ring 3" in New Hampshire would get you somebody's grandma near Mount Washington. All long-distance calls were operator-assisted because, though area codes existed at the call

---

3. Bell Labs was also a ready reserve of smart people the Department of Defense often drew upon; e.g., it developed and implemented the Navy's excellent underwater sound submarine detection system; and it rendered the impartial informed opinion necessary to convince DoD that a nuclear-powered airplane, properly shielded, wouldn't fly. Later in the decade two immigrants, Muhamed Atalla and Dawon Kahng at "The Labs" improved on the original transistor with the invention of the MOSfet (Metal Oxide Semiconductor field effect transistor), the most produced patented invention in world history, the one that made printed circuits possible. Bell Labs later lost its protection from Wall Street's demands in an antitrust suit and, in a diminished state, has been sold to a French company.

centers of AT&T (a monopoly then, remember), they were only being rolled out slowly to homes.

Likewise, postal zip codes were in the future. Recall that in 1962's hit, *Return to Sender*, Elvis sang of "no such number, no such *zone*."

When members of '60 were born, 90% of farms didn't have electricity (stringing lines to remote individual locations was not economically justified for private industry) but by 1950 80% of farms had been wired due to a federal electrification program. Many rural families spoke of the "day the lights went on."

TVs entered some urban future Mids' homes in the 1949-50 time period. Those black and white TVs were rendered large and heavy by cathode ray tubes and hot and unreliable by vacuum tube circuitry. Yet they had brought coverage of the Korean War, the 1952 political conventions, and the 1954 Army-McCarthy hearings to homes without most of the intervening editorial judgment that had shaped news just a few years before. By 1955, the year before '60 was inducted, 50% of American households still did not have TV. The first color broadcasts happened in December of 1953 but the expense of the home sets and the limited number of programs broadcast in color had a mutually reinforcing effect that slowed color's growth. Networks didn't get to 50% color broadcasts until the mid-1960s.

TV sports were, at best, a local phenomenon though by the mid-50s their popularity was cutting into minor league baseball attendance. Pro football was also mostly a matter of local interest. That didn't change until the dramatic, nationally televised (though blacked out in New York), overtime victory of the Baltimore Colts over the New York Giants at the end of 1958. Navy's Heisman winners Bellino and Staubach were yet to star, but the long-term effect of that game on Navy's football success was not positive as young athletes who might previously have chosen a life of military service were lured away by the TV-fueled wealth offered by professional sports. The first broadcast of videotape replays wasn't until 1963, the Army-Navy game in Staubach's Heisman year.

By 1956 the *Happy Days* years of Brylcreem grease, DA haircuts, and poodle skirts were underway. Bill Haley and His Comets had brought new music to teenagers in 1954 but that music didn't hit the charts in any significant way until 1955 when adults heard it as the theme music for *Blackboard Jungle*.[4] In those days grownups bought most records; kids didn't have much money.

Yet the parents who did not have cars before the war were buying new ones every 3 to 6 years and kids might get hand-me-downs or, more likely, through part

---

4. By 1956 Elvis had arrived; he had five of the top twenty records of that year including Heartbreak Hotel. But on '60's induction day the number one song was a memorable one from an artist who, but for that song, would be long forgotten: Gogi Grant's *Wayward Wind* (see the video at https://tiny.cc/ca0-1 or scan QR0-1 on page 8).

time jobs and shared resources, get and rebuild, tune up, and 'chop and channel' a pre-war Ford, Chevy, or Dodge. You know that from *American Graffiti* but stating it here serves the time-gap theme of this chapter.

Virtually all the cars on the nation's roads were built in the USA by domestic manufacturers. Things like radios, heaters, and outside mirrors were "options." When the 1954 Ford Fairlane included seatbelts as standard, its sales dropped sharply and the industry ran the other way, though some offered seat belts as a non-advertised option. The year 1955 saw a 40% boom in car sales stimulated by new designs and more powerful engines. The '55 Chevy remains an icon today. On the June Monday when the bulk of the class of 1960 was sworn in, the last true Packard rolled off the assembly line.

The first Edsel was two years away; the first Toyota dealership about the same.

Cars were one thing but roads were another. On the day that most '60's Mids were inducted, the nation had not one mile of the now 49,000 mile Interstate Highway system. President Eisenhower, still in his first term, signed the law authorizing that system at the end of that week. That bill, with 90% federal funding (91% if the state outlawed billboards along the Interstates) proved an economic boon to the South where local tax bases could not support construction of roads the equal of New York's Thruway and parkways, or the New Jersey or Pennsylvania Turnpikes.

The movements for federal auto safety regulations or, for that matter, environmental regulations, had not begun. Ralph Nader's *Unsafe at Any Speed* and Rachel Carson's *Silent Spring* had yet to be written.

In 1956, other than in military service, most of '60's parents had never flown. If they had, even in the most modern craft, that plane had been built by Lockheed (the three-tailed Constellation) or Douglas (the DC-7). Both were pulled through the air by propellers. The Boeing 707 was 2 years in the future.

In 1956 as the class of 1960 Mids raised their right hands, earth's only satellite was the moon.

The national minimum wage was $1 an hour, raised from 75¢ an hour just the year before. One dollar might seem small, and it was, but in terms of purchasing power it would be worth $9.43 today. The current federal minimum wage is worth 23% less, $7.25. Some of the Midshipmen who entered in 1956 at a salary of $111.15 per month earned more than their parents, particularly if they were from coal country. And a disproportionate share of the class was. Fully 1% of USNA's total enrollment was from one northeastern Pennsylvania coal country county where teens and their parents saw football—particularly service academy football—as a ticket away from the mines.

A chartered bus brings Mids home to the Scranton Area

These are the basic references for a sense of general change from then to now. Other exterior-to-USNA changes will be mentioned as we go on. Yet some significant ones were already underway. In 1955 the U.S. had pledged to support a new government in South Viet Nam that had determined to renege on its 1954 treaty promise of free unification elections in 1956. And in mid-1956 Dr. King's first non-violent protest, the Montgomery bus boycott, was in full swing.

There are other comparisons best described by statistics, not words. Here are a few:

In 1956 the United States was a nation of 169 million people. Its four most populous states were, in order: New York, California, Pennsylvania, and Illinois. In 2020 the United States is a nation of about twice as many people, 329 million, and its four most populous states, in order are: California, Texas, Florida, and New York.

In 1956 the U.S. had an armed force of 2.935 million people of whom 35,000 were women. In 2020 it has an armed force of less than half that, 1.4 million people, of whom 16.5%, or 213,000, are women.

In 1956 the nation had 5 service academies, 3 of which were military,[5] 1 of which, Air Force, was three years away from graduating its first class.

In 1956, when the class of 1960 was inducted, the Navy had a list of 973 ships.[6]

---

5. Counting the Coast Guard as part of the Department of the Treasury as it was then.
6. The list was headed by 3 battleships, 22 attack aircraft carriers, mostly Essex and Midway

When the class of 2020 was inducted the Navy had a list of less than a third of that, 275 ships.[7]

Beyond the Navy over the years between '60's induction and '20's graduation there have been major changes in the American economy.[8] For example, on '60's induction day the Dow Jones Industrial Average closed at 486.43 on a daily share volume on the NYSE of 1.5 million. On the day 2020 graduated the DJIA closed at 24,465.16 on volume (of NYSE stocks traded on all exchanges—something not permitted by the NYSE in 1956) of 3,953.8 million.

Things have changed in terms of income distribution as well. Many more people have significant income and wealth, but the distribution has changed dramatically. In 1950 a CEO made, on average, 20 times the average worker in that company. In 2018 Forbes reported on the disappearing middle class and said that in 2017 the average CEO of a company in the Standard & Poor's 500 average made 361 times the average rank-and-file worker in his or her company. The 5 with the greatest multiple made over 1000 times their average worker. Tax and other legal changes have magnified the income and wealth distribution differentials.

The story in the Navy is different. In 2020 the base pay of an Admiral with 30 years' seniority is 7.6 times the salary of a Seaman with 2 years' seniority, less than the ratio that existed in 1956, 10.9.

Enough already with the numbers.

We want to get to describing the details of the lives of our two classes while they were Midshipmen. But before we do we figure grads would want us to describe the campus and its changes where those lives were lived.

QR0-1

tiny.cc/ca0-1

---

class (Forrestal and Saratoga had been launched but not commissioned though Forrestal's shape and hull number were already on the class of '59's crest), 16 cruisers, 250 destroyers and 108 submarines. Of these ships only 2 were nuclear powered—both submarines. None of its ships had anti-aircraft or ballistic missiles.

7. The list was headed by 10 aircraft carriers, 22 cruisers, 63 destroyers, and 70 submarines (52 attack, 14 ballistic missile, and 4 guided missile). Nuclear power was common. While the destroyers in 1956 had steam power, the current versions are powered by diesel or gas turbine.

8. In 1956 one of today's noted industries, the retail financial industry, essentially didn't exist. Sure, there was a New York Stock Exchange and an American Stock Exchange, but NASDAQ was 15 years in the future and listed options on the Chicago Board came about 10 years after that.

1 FACILITIES

Status quo ante.

When the Class of 1960 arrived in the summer of 1956, the campus was a lot different than it is now. But not much had changed from this, the earliest aerial photo we have found, probably as early as 1916.

AN AIRPLANE VIEW OF THE UNITED STATES NAVAL ACADEMY, ANNAPOLIS, MARYLAND

There were a few changes. Readers who were there in the late '50s are invited to try to pick out the differences. We'll give a list of those we have found in a footnote at the end of this chapter.

We prepared a more extensive reminder of how it was when '60 arrived that summer but, frankly, for a casual reader unfamiliar with the school, that sort of thing is confusing and dull. Yet there are some things even someone who has only heard the word "Annapolis" might find helpful as we go on. So we will start with those.

Appropriately, the best picture we have found of the condition when '60 arrived is one taken in 1956 but saved with an added outline of Christmases Yet to Come, the landfill project that would progress through '60's 3/C and 2/C years.

In June of 1956 the campus was much as intended when it was laid out in Ernest Flagg's 1897 design. At the seaward end there was the dormitory, Bancroft Hall, flanked by buildings for athletics and professional instruction. At the landward end of the campus were the buildings devoted to more usual collegiate academic instruction. The two clusters were joined by a straight, broad, brick-paved pedestrian superhighway, Stribling Walk. We will mention its importance later.

Stribling Walk's west end is at Maryland Avenue. Across the Avenue was and is the academic complex. To head further west, as Mids do on the way to the parade ground, Worden Field, one has to follow Decatur Road which starts from Maryland Avenue, offset a bit to the left from Stribling.

In 1956 that street was particularly memorable for two olfactory reasons experienced by all those who marched along it toward a formal parade.

On Decatur Road, on the left, heading toward Worden, where a parking structure has recently replaced a parking lot, there was a structure sharply differing in architectural merit from all the other structures on campus. It was large, metal, and about as stylish as a huge galvanized milk box.[1] It was part of the water supply system. Apparently the school got its water from wells deep beneath that point. The water was brought to the surface and cascaded, open air, over a series of metal shelves to aerate it. By "aerate it" we mean "allow the stinking hydrogen sulfide to off-gas." Ugh!

---

1. Oh, sorry, we mean what '60 knew as a milk box, a lidded contraption on one's porch where, in a '60 Mid's youth, the milk man picked up the glass bottle empties and left the bottles of fresh milk, homogenized or not.

Worse yet, that area marked the beginning of a stretch of road where USNA (apparently with the naiveté of the fabled king showing off his new clothes) proudly showed off gifts it had received from Japan (before Pearl Harbor, though the gift may have secretly shown the donor's latent animosity). The street was lined with gingko trees. Gingkoes, unlike most trees, are heterosexual; there are male trees and female trees. The ostensibly thoughtful (but arguably malevolent) Japanese had given the school both. In the fall, fertilized female trees drop soft, tan, cherry-sized fruit. We didn't know about the claimed mind-boosting properties of the tree (think *ginko biloba* supplements like Ginkoba).[2] What we did know is that, unlike civilians walking down that street's sidewalks who could avoid the unpleasantness, we who had to march in rank and file through the litter of this fruit could not avoid the sensory equivalent of tromping across the wet floor of a long unswept kennel. The trees remain largely by forbearance (or timidity) of some like one of your authors. See, Pranks, *infra*.

A major change during '60's 2/C year, but off campus about a mile and a half away, was the opening of the privately funded Navy Marine Corps Memorial Stadium. Its name included "Memorial," Mids were told, to allow contributions to be tax deductible. It officially opened for football in '60's final year, but unofficially it had opened for the year before, a lightweight football game.[3] President Eisenhower attended and sat amid the Brigade. The stadium's "Memorial" idea is borne out in lettering along the lower and upper façades of the stands that record memorable events of Naval History since 1900. Among them now are now 5 events commended to memory where members of '60 served.

To save your time and our space we're not going to include pictures of the individual changes in those 56 years. The class of '56 did a fine job of this when it assembled photos taken over the years and posted them on the web in what is essentially a slide show.[4]

One change since '60's time that was always out of sight but is not out of memory deserves respectful mention. The Naval Academy Dairy (which in '60's time provided the Brigade with a couple of gallons of milk for every 12-man table at every meal—and ice cream at one meal each day of the week that contained a "u"[5]) was shuttered in 1998.

All in all, by the time we came to start this book it was getting to look from the air to old-timers that there was no place left on the campus for a raindrop to land on

---

2. We couldn't believe anyone would ever have been the first to ingest the berries and so discover those properties. Our fact checking for this effort revealed that the properties are attributed to the leaves, not the berries. That had to be so.
3. Then called "150-lb football" now called "sprint football."
4. b.link/ca1-1 (or scan QR1 on p. 13)
5. Even occasionally, from 1959 on, for breakfast—with strawberries.

anything but a roof.

In all this discussion of facilities we have not discussed the most important facility. It deserves its own chapter. That's next.[6]

QR 1-1

b.link/ca1-1

---

6. As promised at the outset of this chapter, here are the changes we have noted that existed at '60's induction day and that do not appear on the 1918 photo. Ward Hall next to Dahlgren (Ordnance & Gunnery); The Natatorium next to Macdonough; The "T" extension of the mess hall seaward; Hubbard Hall (the crew team's boathouse); Hospital Point athletic field and its radio telescope and footbridge; the 24 tennis courts; and, Bancroft's 1st and 2nd wings. Even the steel stands at the now long-gone football field were not there yet.

BANCROFT AS A FACILITY

Whether Bancroft Hall, the Academy's dormitory, is still the world's largest dormitory seems to be up for debate.[1] Known as "Mother B" to the classes of 1960 and 2020 and probably a hundred other classes since it was opened in 1906, it has always housed the entire Brigade, even in the years when the Brigade swelled to 4600.

We will start this chapter with facts everyone in the early classes knows well but may welcome a reminder. In any event, those in the current classes may need some basis for comparison as this old building has changed.

In 1956, Bancroft was comprised of 6 wings. They were numbered, as they are today, with the odd-numbered wings on your left and the even on your right as you entered the massive but freely operating front doors. Each matching pair had a different shape.

Each wing nominally had 5 stories, denominated decks, and numbered 0-4. Those stories held the dormitory rooms and offices for 6 battalions and 24 companies.

---

1. On the web you can find support for it being the largest. But one official map of the Yard says only that it is "One of the largest." Another says it is the largest in the nation. The Guinness folk apparently have not taken a stand. The question to their website about world's largest dormitory returns an answer about a camel; an email explaining the unsatisfactory website answer returns a promise of an answer within two weeks; when it comes it is a reference to the website. Perhaps, the consumption of their primary product has rendered the Guinness folk unable to distinguish a dormitory from a dromedary.

(There were central offices in the ceremonial core.)

When it was home to the class of 1960, it held the 3600 midshipmen of all four classes. The Mids roomed with classmates, generally two or three to a room. Each room was located in an area devoted to a company of about 130 men from all four classes. Each company area was located in the same wing as the other three companies in its battalion.

At the end of each academic year those who would be returning the following year normally remained in the same company.[2] They chose their roommates and then they chose their rooms on a class seniority basis and, within each class, by lottery. Plebes could request roommate assignments, usually friends they had made during plebe summer, but only if they had chosen to study the same foreign language.

'60's standard rooms were (by the measurement of memory) roughly 14' feet square (including the entry, closet,[3] and shower) with 12' ceilings. The architects of Bancroft had penciled in some non-standard rooms,[4] particularly above entrances, on the top floor, and other areas rendered non-standard by considerations of exterior necessities or aesthetics. Each room had a sink and its own 3' x 3' stall shower served with hot (scalding hot) and cold water. Each room's shower had a ceiling light. Alternating rooms were designed so their showers were back to back.

Out in the corridor, covering the space where the shower walls backed, was a flimsy full height door (locked but easily opened) designed to provide access to the pipes should the need for a plumbing repair arise. Mids found more uses for these doors and the vertical pipe chases they covered than the architects ever envisioned. Alcohol and later TV storage were probably the most common. But some gave access to attic-like voids where for-money card games were, at least, possible.

One unfortunate Mid was climbing up one of these pipe chases when his foot pressed on an aging pipe or valve and broke it. He was trapped overnight above the spray of near-boiling-point hot water. Worse yet, the water was cascading down and into the Commandant's office. Not his best day.

---

2. Over the years there has been a constant concern over the fact that the upper classes' initial impression of a Mid locks in his or her important "Grease" grade (whether it be called "aptitude for the service" or "military order of merit") for four years. This initial impression by those who will continue to grade each Mid leaves little room for giving effect to his or her improvement as a potential naval officer through his acceptance of the training he or she is receiving. Keeping a Mid with the same upperclass (that is, evaluating) folks leaves the system effectively blind to increases in merit (basically, maturity). Many company and individual rotation and dispersal plans have been tried to counter this effect. The result is that the stay-in-one company for 4 years model is not common, but the system seems to change every year or two.

3. Which held hanging garments such as each Mid's overcoat; reefer (no, not that, a P-jacket with brass buttons), as well as each occupants' shoes, rifle, and bayonet belt set.

4. Up to 2-doored, 5-man rooms.

And that's just the architecture as it probably looked on Mother B's "as built" drawings. Rumor had it that some '60 Mids made two rooms into an even larger suite. Armed with appropriate lumber, plaster, dark green trim paint, and a sledgehammer they connected two existing rooms by an internal doorway. (Most wings—excluding the 5th—had a tradition of annually rotating companies vertically so that no Mid had to spend his 4 years climbing stairs while brethren in the same Battalion went 4 years without climbing any. As a consequence, renovations such as we have described could be pulled off if done early enough in the term that the company officer who had served the previous year on another deck didn't yet know the original layout.)

The walls in all rooms were plastered and painted the ubiquitous middle green the government seems fond of. (Do the paint companies, perhaps out of embarrassment, give it away?) As for the plaster, thermal cycling through many years had persuaded much of the top coat to become estranged from the base coat. The walls in each room had areas where the plaster was blistered beneath the paint and other large areas where it had totally fallen off taking the paint with it. That left broad white areas which, in total effect, made the rooms seem decorated with a fresco of a pinto pony's hide rendered in green and white. But, hey, it made each room unique in a place where anything other than uniformity was longed for but anathema.

The ceilings were painted white and seemed to have avoided the plaster separation plague raging below. Solidly mounted on the ceiling, but suspended a few inches, was a large rectangular light fixture holding long fluorescent bulbs. The bulbs were shielded by a light diffusing panel—glass or plastic, we don't know which. We'll return to that fixture when we discuss pranks.

The standard furniture included 2 metal beds (racks), one of which might be an up and down bunk bed. The room had as many metallic clothes lockers as it had occupants. The bunks, desks, and lockers (which, in defiance of what they were called, could not be locked) were colored dark olive drab at the time of manufacture. The metallic desks, often a double and a single, had dull black linoleum tops. The floors ("decks"), both in the rooms and in the corridors ("passageways"), were paved with 12" square maroon tiles, probably also linoleum.

'60's Mids swept the rooms daily with push brooms, pushing the dust and under-bed blue blanket lint (elsewhere known as "dust bunnies," then and there, with less than reverent reference to Genesis 3:19 "...and unto dust thou shall return.." as "ghost txxxs [i.e., leavings]") out into the corridor. They also put their waste baskets—locally denominated as "shit cans"—out daily. The baskets were emptied and the sweepings swept even further away, by civilian employees, uniformly men of color.

But Bancroft was quite a bit more than bedrooms and a dining facility, the usual stock of a dormitory at any school. Most of the "more" was located on the unnumbered but largely above grade basement level.

At the base of the 6th wing there was a substantial medical clinic (sick bay; now known as the Brigade Medical Organization or BMO). It provided annual physicals, dispensed immunizations, and provided 24/7 medical diagnosis and treatment. The clinic included a 10-bed care facility, though it referred most people needing a medical bed to the on-base hospital.

Adjacent to the sickbay was a fully-staffed 16-chair dental facility. A dental exam was part of the annual physical. Anything revealed during the exam which required treatment (or even marginally justified treatment that could be part of the training of the young dentists) would be scheduled by the facility which would then send a form notice of the appointment to the Mid. The notice would have a handwritten number in a top corner specifying which chair. (If you saw a "16," and knew the code, that was how you learned you were to see Dr. Rodriguez for an extraction.)

This is as good a place as any to mention that the class of 1960 received special dental attention. At the beginning of its plebe academic year its members were asked to be guinea pigs for a major, serious, double-blind toothpaste test. By merely signing a consent form they were promised free toothpaste for their entire four years. Those who agreed (and that was most if not all) received, once a month, a free tube of toothpaste, unidentified save for the bold letter on the box and tube. Apparently, it was a test—probably sponsored by Procter & Gamble—of the efficacy of fluoridated toothpaste. The results were positive and Crest destroyed Colgate's long-term dominance as #1 in sales.[5] (Those who got "Toothpaste G" swear they were in the control group and their product was made with sugar-acid concentrate. Annual double-digit fillings at school led to a life-time of filling replacements. But, hey, it was for a good cause.)

The lowest level of the 6th wing also held Bancroft's post office which is now in the 7th wing and now has its own zip code, 21412.

The 6th wing's counterpart, the 5th, had on its ground floor a full-sized industrial dry cleaning plant. It handled at least 4,000 blue woolen uniforms, pairs of slacks, and gabardine shirts a week, returning them smelling of more than a modicum of imbedded, aromatic perchlorethylene. The ground level of the 5th wing also housed meeting rooms near a side entrance to the mess hall where dinner meetings of various activities hosted their often significant guests (e.g., the Spanish Club with the Spanish Ambassador, or the Political Economy Club with Chairman Burns of the Council of Economic Advisors or Senator Muskie of the Senate Finance Committee). The 5th's

---

5. What a great choice for a scientific study. Here was a totally captive, sure to get a dental exam every year, cohort of a statistically valid size, composed of folks in prime cavity years. We wondered whether the class of '60, USMA, participated in a similar test. According to LCOL Bob Totten, an Association of Graduates, USMA class of '60 contact, it did not.

ground floor was also configured to serve the loading docks required by the kitchen.

Scattered about the various wings' ground floors, including the 5th, were 4 barber shops averaging 6 chairs each.

The ground floor of the 3rd wing sheltered the Midshipmen's store, then with an inventory pretty much limited to toiletry products and replacements for items issued on I-Day, hats, underwear, sweatshirts, shoes, socks, collars for white shirts,[6] etc. Of course shoe polish was a hot item—the Brigade was split between Mids religiously loyal to Kiwi and those who swore by Griffin's Microsheen. It did not offer the competitive brand oft-mentioned as not detectibly different from a lesser substance, Shinola.

The ground floor of the 4th wing housed a couple of set-em-up-yourself bowling alleys, a rifle range, and the band room. The bowling alleys are no longer there. Instead there are spaces for various musical groups, including the Drum & Bugle Corps, to store their instruments and practice. There are also rooms for several other clubs, a room for repair and replacement of CAC cards, the pass cards Mids now use to get into Bancroft, a computer repair shop, varsity squash courts and locker rooms, the offices and shop for the Facilities staff, etc.

They say meat packers use every part of the hog but the oink. So too those who planned the utilization of the square footage of the ground level of Bancroft. Apparently, the open-to-the-air but totally enclosed center courtyards within the 3rd and 4th wings" box-like layouts offended their sense of spatial frugality. So they filled them with wood frame structures containing squash and handball courts. They now contain infrastructure machinery, mostly part of the air conditioning system added in 2006.

The ground level of the central, ceremonial, section of Bancroft housed the snack and milk shake-serving facility known as "Steerage" beneath the formal entry Rotunda. On the same level but beneath Memorial Hall was Smoke Hall, the location of the only regulation TV in the building and the exclusive domain of first classmen.

For all four of '60's years each Mid put his laundry in a white canvas, name-stenciled bag. He placed it in the corridor on a set day, once a week. It was picked up there, processed in the plant next to Dorsey Creek, and returned, folded, about a week later.

With the laundry plant gone, for the classes such as 2020, things are different, as you would expect. For plebes things are somewhat comparable; there are large carts

---

6. The shirts worn with dress blues called for separate collars that had to be attached, fore and aft. Originally, they were linen. In the last year or two of '60's tenure the linen ones were replaced with stiff disposable paper ones. The stiffness effect of the shirt collars in the khaki uniform was achieved through the use of a wire and spring contraption, a "Spiffy."

delivered to each company deck. There is a daily cycle that amounts to once a week pickup with a one-week turnaround. They have two netted laundry bags and one large fabric bag. Colors go in the yellow netted bag and whites in the white netted bag. Then both are added to the large fabric bag along with towels and linens. Mids fill out a short form marking one yellow and one white netted bag and how many towels and linens are in the larger bag.

Now plebes put uniforms that require dry cleaning in a separate blue bag that looks like a suit cover when stretched flat. This bag gets its own form to track the uniforms.

The blue uniform bags and white fabric bags are then carted to a large truck and taken to a laundry facility near the heating plant. This is on King George St. across from the baseball stadium but not within the campus walls. The netted bags are washed on high heat without removing the clothes. Athletic wear and clothes you don't care much about can withstand this treatment but they come back crumpled. Any civvies included come back quite ruined. On delivery day, it is the responsibility of the 4th class to deliver laundry to the upper class.

Most upperclass don't use this service. For them there is access to two self-service laundry rooms (think coin operated laundromat but with credit card readers) in 5th and 4th wing basements. They have to pay for these but it is very affordable and doesn't ruin their clothes. The only downside is competing for an empty washing machine or dryer since they are always in use. The Facilities people have installed cameras in the laundry rooms, gyms, and the barber shop so all can tune in and see a live video stream of how busy places are before actually going down.

Other features of Bancroft known to 2020 and unknown to 1960 include a bank, a shoe repair shop, and a tailor shop. Did the Administration in the '50s think Mid's shapes were not going to change in their 4 years or did they just think that if the school stretched out the issuance of uniforms at least one of the uniforms would fit? And, because required by the increased diversity of courses offered, there is now a bookstore in the 5th wing basement where formerly the formal dinners were held; they have moved to the 4th wing.

Of course, like many college dormitories, Bancroft had a dining facility, a mess hall. It was accessible in the center of the building by stairs down from Smoke Hall or, from the side wings, by ramps down from the ground level of the 5th and 6th wings. It was truly part of Bancroft, but it deserves its own chapter which we'll get to in a bit. But first we'll pick up with the description of the lives led by our 2 classes within and around these facilities, starting with Plebe Summer.

PLEBE SUMMER

PLEBE SUMMER IS THE ACADEMY'S VERSION OF BOOT CAMP JUST AS Beast Barracks is West Point's version of Army Basic.

On Monday, June 25, 1956 USNA welcomed the class of 1960 with the usual: forms to be signed, haircuts, physicals, and issuance of work uniforms. These days, the day of arrival is called Induction Day, shorthanded to "I-Day." That term was not used in 1956, but it's handy and we'll use it for both classes.

Uniforms issued that day included the basic summer work uniform "whiteworks" shown in two modifications in the photos below. These photos are of current issue. They show plastic name plates; members of the class of 1960 ink-stenciled their names across their uniforms' chest. In part we are including these photos here because the terms "whiteworks," "Dixie cups," and "Caps" come up often in these pages and some readers may not be familiar with them. The Mid wearing the Cap is on the left, the one wearing the Dixie cup (and athletic shoes and tee shirt) is on the right.

Besides being taught to salute and to march in step, the class of 1960 spent a fair amount of its first day with stencils, black ink, and brushes applying their names to the hats, work uniforms, skivvies, laundry bags and probably a lot more.[1] With limited exception the entire class of '60 was sworn in that day.

'60's youngest member was an exception to the mass swearing in. To qualify, candidates had to be over 17 by July 1, and under 26 by their projected graduation date. He made the age cut off by almost 4 days but on I-Day was not yet 17. So his Company Officer, an Army exchange officer, Captain George ("Treadhead" or "Tanktracks") Patton, son of WWII's famed General Patton and destined to be a general in his own right, wouldn't let him take the oath. The one-of-a-kind classmate watched from a Bancroft window.

Others who did not participate in the mass swearing in were those who had been bused in from NAPS, the Naval Academy Preparatory School. They had been sworn in the day before.

The last exception known to us was a group of people whose admission had not yet been confirmed. They held alternate appointments. Many of them had hopes dampened the day after I-Day when newspapers around the country printed the annual I-day photo of a future defensive lineman standing next to a future crew coxswain in their new uniforms. (The cliché annual photos still emphasize size differences, but now also pick people of different gender. '60's picture was a tad unprecedented as the class was the first not limited to 6'4" in height; its limit was 6'6".) In those days the admissions people at USNA counted how many of those accepted actually showed up to be sworn in, compared that with how many the school wanted, and issued telegraphic invitations to that number of qualified alternates. So it was that a goodly number of athletes—and a few folks who were not—arrived and went through the I-Day rituals on one of the following two Mondays. *(Jack - I was among them, decidedly a "were not;" one who would now be called a NARP, a Non-Athletic Regular Person.)*

I-Day for the class of '20, and those closely before and after it, was considerably different than '60's.[2] For one thing, each induction day is videoed by the Public Affairs Office, edited, narrated, and posted on the web. The video of '20's I-Day is still available there at this writing at tiny.cc/ca3-1 (QR3-1 on p. 30) and will remain

---

1. It was also issued individual "plebe bibles"—*Reef Points*. This small (approximately 3" x 5" x 1") volume contained an enormous amount of info that had to be memorized. It was also destined to become the core component of a Plebe's "plebe kit," a plastic-wrapped accumulation of one of everything an upper classman might of an instant require from a Band-Aid to a needle and thread (black and white) to... well, you name it. The kit was always carried in the plebe's garter-supported sock at his ankle, about where a policeman keeps his backup weapon.

2. It was even more different from the day of arrival at colleges other than a military academy. This was not a 'parents drive you up and help you bring your stuff to your room' experience. Anything a new Mid might bring or wear, other than his toothbrush, is to be put in a bag and sent home. He might as well put his toothbrush in the bag because he'd be issued a couple of them too.

available in the Nimitz Library collection.[3] Now I-day starts at Alumni Hall where most who are accompanied by parents or friends are dropped off to go through most of the day by themselves. Then, as part of the "Another Link in the Chain" program, the parents (etc.) who choose to stay are hosted by members of the class from 50 years earlier. The parents next see their uniformed, militarily haircut, offspring marching in step at the end of the day, filing in to the swearing-in ceremony pictured above on page 2.

One difference a '60 grad would notice if he followed the new arrivals through the day is that the new plebes are not issued the most worn issued item from his time, the Navy bathrobe, a "b-robe."

Once sworn in, '60 was divided into "crews" of roughly 15 and assigned, 3 to a room, in a string of adjoining rooms.

Jack - My experience wasn't unique in this regard, but I was in with a truly admirable group of guys. One of my roommates made Navy a career and retired as a Captain. The other, an all-state football player in high school, realized in the first semester that he wasn't ever to be on Navy's varsity. He decided he'd rather be a big fish in a smaller pond, intentionally flunked the Chemistry mid-term, and left for his home state's university. Nonetheless his interest in service had been genuine; he made the military his career and retired as an Army general.

Each person from my summer crew went on to have stories worth telling—some from school, e.g., Navy football, or basketball, or Olympic teams—some not. One of my favorites is told by a crew mate who was in Kuwait City leading a sales mission for a defense contractor when Sadam's tanks rolled into town. His efforts to save his team from capture and the harrowing night (and days) after they were captured could keep Tom Clancy writing for weeks. Another from our crew, long our class president, injured his knee as a lineman on Navy's varsity football team. It didn't hold up to service on an escort destroyer and he became our only retired-as-an-ensign classmate. Yet he went on to command a larger fleet than anyone else in our class, Exxon's international tanker fleet.

Though it's outside the scope of this attempt at a light-hearted look at change, at this point decency compels a mention that in other crews assembled that summer other stories of greater weight were yet to unfold. Many were of the type you might expect: Navy Crosses and Silver Stars earned; Command of fleets in peace time and

---

3. We have checked with Dr. Jennifer Bryan, archivist at the Nimitz Library, and she has confirmed that the video in all YouTube postings by the Public Affairs Office are permanently archived at Nimitz and will survive any "outdated" delisting from YouTube.

of a Marine Division in battle; success in individual mortal aerial combat; ejections over enemy territory; lives cut short by even peacetime demands of the service—military aircraft, submarines, surface ships, and infantry operations are dangerous. Other stories were written in American commerce, particularly in the nuclear power industry in which members of the class of '60 figured prominently. Here those stories are an aside, but in the hearts of members of the class, they are central.

Members of the class of '20 have stories yet to be written so comparisons today are impossible. But in years to come it is inevitable that those stories will be worth the telling.

But whatever the story, in '60's plebe summer all that was in the future.

'60's Plebe Summer was managed by a pack (maybe 30, at most 40) of newly-minted Ensigns from the class of '56, and it was held on an otherwise almost empty campus. Most often the Ensigns were those who had selected Navy Air so, instead of going to sea, they were awaiting their spot to open at Pensacola. It was their job to conduct plebe summer, the Academy's equivalent of boot camp.

The only event outside USNA that was brought to '60's attention during that summer was the late July collision of two cruise ships, the *Andrea Doria* and *Stockholm*. The *Doria* sank the next day.

'20's Plebe summer was ruled by an extensive and more hyper upper class Plebe Summer Detail. For a sense of the size of that detail consider this photo of 2020's swearing-in on page 2 above. The Mids standing, two and sometimes three deep, like prison guards at each end of the seated rows, were that Detail.

And the campus during 2020's plebe summer held a lot more people than '60's had. Those people included Mids, to be sure, and not just those on the Summer Detail. They included Mids in voluntary or involuntary summer school or involved in summer programs of upperclass years that required their presence on campus including sailing, powered flight, YP (yard patrol craft) Squadron, and nearby internship programs. Others aboard included those in programs designed to familiarize high school students with the USNA lifestyle, some in academic STEM classes and others varsity sports camps.

'60's days that summer were devoted to lacing on leggings and marching, lacing and marching,[4] and lac..., well you get the point.

---

4. Some never-been-in-the-military stand-up comedian is probably making a living mocking the military for training humans that have been walking for at least 16 years, and standing even longer, to walk and stand in a box-like formation that hasn't been useful in combat since shortly after the Etruscans taught it to the Romans. Such a comic never stood on Worden Field trying hard with all the fellows around him to make their unit look good and learned the lesson of the itch. That's when the inevitable itch on your nose hits and grows more maddening as you realize that scratching it will be an act of disloyalty to your colleagues. That's when you learn loyalty to the collective effort on a very personal level.

There were also such things as machine shop (casting, metal lathe work, and such all to the end of manufacturing a threaded, drilled-out stuffing box bolt about the size of a softball). '60 also spent time learning to sail, taking a short course in mechanical drawing, and dis-and re-assembling a 1937 Cadillac engine.

The class also had two hours of introductory training in each of God knows how many sports many had never played before—handball, squash, tennis, crew, golf, and such. Besides sailing and crew, the class also hit the water to row 10-oared long boats to learn teamwork.

Our words are not the best way to learn about 2020's plebe summer. For that we commend another YouTube video, which you can see at tiny.cc/ca3-2 (or scan QR3-2 on page 30).

Yet our recitation here, speaking to a comparison of the experiences of our two classes may contain some observations not evident on '20's YouTube.

After I-day, '20's summer started off differently. For one thing its members were arriving on a campus where there would be much more academic diversity. Like '60, '20 had a significant contingent of people who had previous collegiate experience. And, similarly, but unlike '60, many of '20s Mids had come from high schools with Advanced Placement courses. Rather than ignoring those experiences as it had in 1956, in 2016 USNA assessed them. It did not automatically honor past experiences but, within the first week or so, it conducted qualification tests for many courses including Calculus I and II, Chemistry I and II, Physics I and II, English Composition, and Language. Success on any one of the tests could exempt a student from a cognate course, qualify him or her for a more advanced course, or even lighten the course load remaining for graduation.

'20 didn't have time in a machine shop. And pulling wooden long boats had morphed into paddling inflatables for the teamwork lessons.

However, its sailing training was much like '60's. '20 learned a bit more sailing in classrooms. But on the water it learned on 26-foot fiberglass, sloop-rigged, keeled boats called "Colgates" carrying 4 mids and an instructor. '60 had learned on 26-foot wooden, sloop-rigged, keeled boats called "knockabouts" carrying 4 mids and an instructor. For both classes the instructors were new Ensigns. For '20 this was welcome relief from the ministrations of the upperclass plebe summer detail.

Both classes had the opportunity to take additional instruction and a test and thus qualify to host guests (girlfriends, parents, high school classmates, etc.) sailing on the Severn during the remainder of their 4 years.

2020's 26-footers are also used for the Junior Varsity Offshore Sailing program and for that they are outfitted with spinnakers. In its Plebe summer '60 had brief exposure to the school's wooden-hulled 44-foot Luders yawls. '20 had nothing comparable though Rob, a sailing enthusiast, had a lot of time on Navy's current fleet of fiberglass hulled, sloop-rigged 44's. That was not typical of his class and it didn't start until spring of his 4/C year. Mids in '60 also did get a turn on some of the school's larger boats including the 98-foot Highland Light, winner of the 1933 Bermuda race, and Freedom, reputedly Hitler's private yacht taken as a prize of war.

In its plebe summer 2020 had considerable damage control training, including donning and clumping about in heavy protective firefighting gear. '60 didn't get to firefighting until a trip in its 2/C summer to the Philadelphia Navy Yard.

Oh, we mentioned 1960's long boats. They were stored, hung by block and tackle, in sheds that are no longer there, above water that is also no longer there, about 50 yards out the Severn-side door of the Mid's Store. '60 Mids had some instruction time at that location standing in the heat of the tarmac with their backs toward Macdonough Hall and their faces toward the only enlisted man[5] that '60 dealt with on the yard in its 4 years, Chief Bo'sun's Mate "Shorty" Metzger. He had so many 4-year service stripes on his dress blues you'd swear they went up one arm and down the other. He taught '60 its knots and the sea-goers' way of pronunciation. For example, the boats were hoisted by "Block and Take–el." It's a "Boy" not a "boo-ey" as landlubbers might think. And when the two pulley things on the hoisting apparatus are in contact the system is said to be "two-blocked" or "chock-a-block."

'20's Mids learned their knots (yes, even in the 21st century knots are essential to shipboard operations and safety) seated in air-conditioned classrooms from people who probably had less time at sea than Chief Metzger had at left full rudder.

The evenings in '60's plebe summer meant a gathering in the Mahan Hall

---

5. Other than Yard Patrol craft crewmen and Mess stewards.

auditorium for a lecture, a military-theme movie,[6] or a group sing to teach the school songs. At least 70% of the lectures included the phrase, "You're only going to get out of this place what you put into it." Many in the audience didn't have the foggiest what the speaker meant. Those speaking may not have known what they meant either. It may have just been on everyone's suggested lesson plan. Maybe the Mids would have come away more motivated if the lecturers had repeatedly said, "We're going to try to make you a better person, morally, mentally and physically. You owe it to your reputation, that of your classmates, and that of the school to get with the program, don't fight it, don't simply endure it, get with it. Work with us to become the person we want you to be. If you're here, it's the also person you want to be."

What '60 did not have in plebe summer, and classes like '20 do have, is an hour and a half every weekday morning participating in class-wide physical workouts. To its credit, the school now puts a lot more effort on the "Morally, mentally, and physically" phrase that has long been embedded in its mission. Being physically fit is not only healthier for the Mids and enables them to better face the physical demands of the service, but it connotes self-discipline and thus quietly connotes authority to those the grads will be called on to lead.

'60 had an obstacle course—qualify once during plebe summer and forget it—in back of Bancroft on ground where buildings now stand. Classes like '20 have a much more elaborate obstacle course and do-stuff-at-heights training across the river.

As all readers from the class of '60 know, "across the river" brings us to rifle range days. In various groups each day of the week that summer a fifth of the class of '60 was motor-launched across the river for a day being drilled on small arms by Marines apparently seeking revenge for their treatment by some drill sergeant past.

The day was invariably extremely hot and as humid as only Tidewater can get. '60 Mids would debark, line up, and double time to some place for instruction—a Quonset hut, sun-broiled to almost car-in-the-summer-parking-lot temperatures, for a how-to-do-something movie, perhaps. Then they'd double time to the next station, the rifle range or the pistol range most likely, as the day got hotter still. And so the day went: a range, more heat, double time, a movie, more humidity, double time, a range, double time, a lecture, double time, a range all day until, with sweat-salted eyes, they double timed back to the boats for the ride back to Bancroft's version of civilization.

Believe it or not, The Farmer's Almanac website has the daily Naval Academy

---

6. Unfortunately, very few of the best WWII movies had been made by then. *12 O'Clock High* had been, but *The Bridge on the River Kwai* was a year away. Incidentally, the week it came to town *The Colonel Bogie March*, which had long been played during the "pass in review" part of formal parades, disappeared from the repertoire in the certain belief it would lead to spontaneous whistling in the ranks.

weather for each day in the summer of 1956. Its memory is different than '60's. Maybe those readings were taken in the shade of the Administration Building on the main campus; they couldn't have been taken in the sun on the other side of the Severn.

While we're on that point, be aware that the school has a different view of the risks of heat stroke these days. The Public Affairs Office's annual YouTube videos of I-Day show plebes marching into Bancroft at the end of their first day with canteens strapped to the small of their backs. And there is an elaborate regulation defining what constitutes a Black Flag Day and what limitations flow from reaching that condition.

The "Flag" conditions are defined by a temperature/humidity measurement on a Wet Bulb Globe Thermometer. The thresholds for the various conditions and the consequence of each are printed on a card given to all who conduct activities at the school from mid-May to mid-September.

Essentially, it imposes no restrictions at wet bulb temperatures below 85° at any time, or below 88° after 3 weeks (a period apparently chosen to allow Alaskans to acclimate to their new semi-tropical Tidewater environment). Then it restricts outdoor physical training above 88° and all outdoor non-aquatic physical activity (e.g. marching drill and rifle range activity) above 90°.

For members of '20, the canteen was an official part of the uniform. They knew that any plebe forgetting his or hers would assuredly be carrying around two or more for several days so as to burn "bring your canteen" into memory. Safety is definitely the first priority. Most from '20 will defend the temperature restrictions with the argument that a broken plebe can't train, so there is inherent value in the rules. Many from '60 who served in 'Nam or the Gulf might say weather is part of the military; get used to it.

The current plebe summer heat and humidity limits, the "flag conditions," only applied outdoors. Since most of the physical training occurred early in the morning or as punishment inside now-air-conditioned Bancroft Hall, there was still plenty of room for physical stress. The physical events outside, such as the obstacle courses, could face delays or cancellations; however, they were usually planned for the morning. Black flag conditions were rarely in effect before noon, so there was enough time for other outdoor training.

But back to the tale of '60's days across the river. The hours weren't entirely devoted to drills and sweat. There was a "break" mid-day for lunch, something nondescript flung from a steam table onto a metal chow hall serving tray and eaten in a sun-heated field. Invariably the tray included a pineapple upside down cake with its obligatory half cherry staring up at the Mids who stared down trying to identify the other stuff on the tray.

'20's days across the river for weapons instruction and obstacle course tasks were likewise broken up by a meal: slug-a-bag-and-it-heats-up MREs. They're officially known as Meals, Ready to Eat, but they are universally and insensitively referred to throughout the U. S. military as Meals Refused by Ethiopians.

For rifle training, '60 fired WWII's standard infantry weapon, the M-1 (Garand) rifle for training and score. And they shot carbines for familiarity. They fired these weapons at targets 200 yards away and alternated rounds of firing with double-timing the 200 yards to "the butts." There they hunkered behind a berm while others of their number fired at the targets above their heads, targets which they hauled down, plugged the hole with a wooden dowel through a cardboard disk of contrasting color to note the score, raised to communicate the score, brought back down to repair the hole, then raised again for the next shot. (One mid, overheard singing the Marine Corps Hymn to the tune of Clementine or Red River Valley was excused from double timing to the butts. He "was allowed" to duck walk to and fro singing the Marine Corps Hymn. He did, but since he was not closely observed, he reportedly continued to use his preferred melody.)

Mids in '60's fired for score toward the end of the summer when they fired from seated cross-legged, kneeling, standing, and prone positions. If a Mid achieved some score (if memory serves it was 230 out of a possible 250) he was awarded an "expert" in rifle ribbon that he could wear on his uniform.

For pistol training, '60 fired Colt 1911 .45s for score and a Thompson submachine gun (which also used the heavy, short-range, stop-a-bayonet-charge, .45 round) for familiarity. When you held that sucker and pulled the trigger you had a devil of a time keeping it aimed at the target as with each round it tried to jump up and to the right while the next round came too soon to correct for the last. (If Capone's crew had as much difficulty with the Thompson, a/k/a the Tommy Gun, as '60's plebes did no one would have been hurt in that garage on St. Valentine's Day.)

'60 was trained to shoot the pistol standing, holding the piece in one hand at full arm's length; the other hand was to be in a pocket or behind the back. Most couldn't help thinking the pose was stylish, to be sure, but friggin' stupid. If Mids were ever going to use a .45 against a similarly armed person of ill will, they were probably going to dive prone to make themselves smaller targets and, while rolling, blaze away. They knew what good just standing there had done for Alexander Hamilton.

When '60 fired pistol for score, it was at ranges of 15 and 25 yards.

In major contrast, all '20's small arms training happened in one day. The day involved a pontoon boat over, weapons introduction, and finally firing for score. The rifle qualification was held shooting the newer M-4 at 25 yards (admittedly with smaller bull's eyes). For pistol qualification, '20 used a two-hand grip to fire a Sig-Sauer 226 (9 mm model) at targets 3, 7 and 15 yards away.

'20's Mids who qualified as experts on either weapon were granted, as qualifying '60 Mids were, "expert" ribbons. '20's ribbons look like the ribbons of the earlier time but now they have a small silver "E" to designate expert status. Others in '20 who posted a lower score were also awarded similar ribbons but with a bronze "S" for Sharpshooter. Still other '20 mids received identical ribbons that had no metallic identification for scoring at the Marksman level. All the ribbons look the same save only that, as noted, some have small metal identifiers too small for the now-aging eyes of '60 to notice at any distance beyond arm's length.

If '60's Mids didn't qualify at the expert level, they didn't get a ribbon.

The overall effect of the more generous ribbon awards—including the issuance of National Defense medals—is that by the time '20 Mids next saw their parents, often at the end of the summer when they were first allowed town liberty, most of them had a full row of laudatory laundry on their chests. Oh, and those chests were clothed in summer whites, not the warmer woolen suit-like dress khakis.

'60's Plebe Summer ended on Labor Day weekend as the upperclassmen returned. In anticipation of that, '60 moved out of their plebe summer rooms and were scattered to various Battalion areas based on the language class they had selected. Most often that meant new roommates.

'20's Plebe Summer assignments proved more durable. Each entering '20 Mid was assigned to a numbered platoon, say the 26th (part of a lettered Plebe Summer company). At the end of the summer that unit, again say the 26th platoon, remained together and merged into the academic year 26th Company.

For '20 the upper classes returned and the Brigade re-formed earlier, around August 17th.

Both classes knew Plebe Summer had been no picnic and they more or less dreaded the upper classes' return. For the class of 1960 that day was uniformly spoken of as "the day the shit hits the fan." For the class of 2020 it was called "Hello Night" but members of that class fully appreciate the earlier nomenclature. Both classes wondered, "How much worse could it get?"

Well, plebe summer was an exception. Let's get on with telling about routine life in the Academic Year in Mother B.

QR3-1

tiny.cc/ca3-1

QR3-2

tiny.cc/ca3-2

DAILY LIFE IN BANCROFT, THEN

LIFE IN BANCROFT FROM 1956 TO 1960 WAS A LIFE SEVERELY BOUND BY rules, by Midshipman Regulations a/k/a "the Regs."

The rules founded on neatness mandated which side of which locker shelf was to hold which of their socks, jocks, skivvies, Dixie cups, and other permitted stuff. The Regs also established where they had to hang their laundry bags. Some classmates took neatness up a notch and simonized their desk tops. Some even went beyond that and simonized their decks (floors, remember). As far as we know, no one repaired the plaster.

The rules also extended to attempts to use décor to express some individuality. Those rules generally said, "Verboten!" Plebes were not allowed pictures of any kind displayed, even in their lockers. 2/C and 3/C were allowed one framed picture in their lockers. First classmen were allowed such a picture, usually of their intended, on their desk.

But remember, we said the rules "generally" forbade individual expression. One exception allowed all, other than plebes, one map per room on the wall. Irrepressible individuality can exploit such an exception. One rumor had it that a prank-prone Mid in the class of '59 wrote the Air Force's Strategic Air Command in Omaha for a copy of its full-wall global map seen behind speakers at press conferences. He got it but apparently his roommates talked him out of his plan to wallpaper their room with it. It was legal perhaps, but unacceptable—probably to the prankster's roommate, a person with the maturity and gravitas to be a future Commander-in-Chief, U.S. Atlantic Fleet.

When '60 escaped plebe-dom and could have their own maps, a more determined member of the class decided to do the prankster one better. He wrote the Soviet Embassy in Washington to ask for a copy of a comparable map from the Soviet Air Force. Unfortunately for him, a letter to that embassy with a USNA return address caught the attention of the FBI team monitoring the embassy's mail. Back in Annapolis, the command was not amused. He was awarded 75 demerits and 30 days of restriction and half- hourly Battalion Office musters when not otherwise scheduled. His junior and senior years were at a different school.

There was a sense that the moment in which a week in Bancroft started to transition into the next week was Sunday evening, after dinner. Sunday evening will be mentioned in the King Hall chapter and the time after Sunday dinner will come up in the Women chapter. Clearly, Sunday evening was different.

On the mundane level, by Sunday evening the selection of barbershop appointments, the first item on the following week's agenda, had to have run its course. Haircuts for the class of 1960 were more than just a photo-op on I-day. The subjective aspects of the disciplinary haircut standard were such that everyone had to have a haircut once a week (the more hirsute, twice). Appointments at a barbershop were required. One person in each company, usually second or third class, had the responsibility to give out rigid composite tiles, each the size of a credit card but about 4 times as thick. Each tile designated the day, time, and location of an appointment. The distributor announced times when he would be available for each class, in order of seniority, to select its tiles. During those times members of the appropriate class would pick, from among the then-remaining tiles, one that best fit his class and medical/dental appointment schedule. It was a given that if he missed his appointment, he'd flunk an inspection and have to march off the consequences.

But, preparatory activities aside, the week truly started on Monday morning. Unless a '60 Mid were marching off some demerits or attending daily Catholic mass (both pre-reveille), his day started at 6:15 with the B-ring-ing-ing of the loudest damn school bell ever made sounding a 10-second blast followed by 10 shorts.[1] Hell, under the *Inland Rules of the Road* a full-throated ship's whistle's "prolonged" and three shorts were enough to alert everyone in every harbor in America that something was

---

1. Jim Webb's *A Sense of Honor* suggests that by his time some self-appointed patriot had decided to change the bell to ring for 13 seconds followed by 13 shorts. By God, if the country started with the number13, so too should every Mid's day! We hope there is a hell for people like that.

changing. Ten shorts seemed a bit much. But it did give time for what '60 Mids were required to do by the time silence returned: get up, remove all their bedding from its tucked-under state and pile it in the middle of the bed (nothing hanging over the edge), and vector one of their number, b-robed, to poke out into the passage and indicate—under penalty of an honor violation—that all occupants had met the bell's command.

'60's Mids then had a half hour before breakfast meal formation to shower, shave, and shine shoes—or for that matter write letters, review class notes, or anything they wanted except to re-make the beds. They couldn't do that until after the meal, though they had to have done it before the bell rang to signal it was time to form up for first period class (even if, individually, they didn't have a first period class). Neither could they lie or sit on the beds until after breakfast; plebes couldn't until taps.

The beds had to be made to military standards, though somewhat below the "bounce a quarter" level of a Marine barracks.

'60 Mids thought their wake-up ritual was remarkably uncivilized until their 2/C year exchange weekend at West Point. Reveille there wasn't a wake up, it was an outdoor fully dressed formation. Their post-wide wake up was an obnoxious "First Call to Reveille."

Back in Bancroft another sleep-time custom was in effect for winter months. First know that back then Bancroft was heated by radiator-delivered steam heat. It was shut off building-wide at night. At 0500 it returned with the loud hammering of slugs of water, condensed in bends of the pipes overnight and slammed into radiators and pipe bends by the rise the of the fresh steam. Most Mids sleeping with their widows open slept through the din. But they didn't want to awake to a still-cold room. So a detail, comprised of plebes from a different room each week, was designated to go into every room in their company and close the windows so the occupants could avoid that unpleasantness. Sleeping upper classmen, who had just proved they could sleep through the audio equivalent of the Anvil Chorus or an artillery barrage, were inordinately sensitive to any misstep by a thus-tasked plebe, and more than moderately grumpy about it.

Another aspect of requirements of plebes in Bancroft was that, in the Hall but outside of their own rooms, plebes had to walk or run eyes straight ahead ("in the boat"), hands rigidly extended ("finned out"), in the center of the corridors ("passageways") and make square corners when turning. On the staircases ("ladders" about the width of those in a typical public high school), they were always to run ("chop") and use only the outermost portion of each tread. Those quartered on the top deck were said to build "legs of redwood" in their first year. (Why redwood, a long enduring but relatively soft species, no one ever explained. Somebody must have figured that out because the race to the 4th deck is now said to build legs of steel.)

Each day a different group of Mids stood watch. The watch day started after evening meal with a serious formal inspection wearing the dress uniform of the season in the Rotunda. Then they were dispatched to their posts. Those posts were either offices or, for underclass, standing at lecterns in the hallways, one per wing per floor, at a point where the watchstander had a view of the main and one intersecting passageway.

Their duties were largely communication: passing along any word relayed to their post by sound-powered phone, updating a chalkboard at their station, distributing the morning copies of the *Washington Post*, delivering the mail, and alerting the Main Office to anything alarming.

The watch was shut down at taps and reinstituted before reveille. Each post was served in two sections with a Mid relieving a colleague at appointed hours.

Watch had priority over classes, but off-duty members of the watch were otherwise at the disposal of the command.

Here's one way that "disposal" was employed. In the '50s, though there were only 3 major TV networks and no cable, shows about the Navy took up a goodly share of the available time. Early in the decade American viewers had watched the 26 30-minute episodes of NBC's richly orchestrated historical documentary, *Victory at Sea*. For a couple of years before the class of '60 was formed, viewers had watched a dramatic series, *Navy Log*, themed by *The Navy Hymn* a/k/a *Eternal Father*. In '60's plebe year, that hole in the networks' schedules was filled by a series, *Men of Annapolis*. It had large segments filmed on location. Off-duty members of the watch section were pressed into service as uncompensated extras on camera, <u>being</u> Mids alongside well-paid actors <u>imitating</u> Mids.

We'll cover the daily drill on meals, classes, athletics, and such in separate sections; this section is about Bancroft. So let us skip ahead to immediately after dinner.

There was a null period before required study, 2000 to 2200. That null was mostly used by upper class, typically second class, hosting plebes on "come arounds." Come arounds were one on one, shall we say, counseling sessions in the upper classman's room for correction of noted substandard appearance or conduct. Others not so engaged used the time for socializing, often playing games of chess, bridge, or poker. For part of the year, some companies used the time to practice reading flashing light Morse code signals (a common form of communication between ships) for that component of the Color Company competition.

After the mandatory study period, the brief 20 minutes before that damn bell signaled taps at 2220 allowed corridor use, resumption of inter-room socialization, and completion of the card games.

For '60's first 3 years, taps meant "lights out." Only 1/C were allowed to study later, but only until 2300. If underclassmen felt they needed to evade the rules and study after 2220, they had to get into the shower, hang their dark blue blanket over the curtain rod as a blackout screen, and turn on the shower light. At 2300 someone with a master switch, probably at the power plant, turned off all power to Bancroft except that needed for safety lighting—about one out of every 5 corridor lights. In those later hours everyone, including first class, studying in the absence of building power had to use flashlights. Obviously, only one Mid per room per day could get in extra study time in the shower.[2]

If you had searched for a reason for these hour restrictions you'd have come up with two, neither official. First, the school didn't care as much about a Mid learning as much as he could as it cared about seeing how much he could learn compared to others in the same time period. Conclusion? Class standing meant more than knowledge. Second, almost all of '60's Mids had to have 20/20 vision to get in. Once in, the school didn't want anyone disqualified for aviation or even sea duty because of eyesight limitations before he came up for commissioning. That's not far-fetched. The English Department didn't have to submit the books it chose to censors for content, but it did have to submit them to the Medical Department for its clearance that the typeface and page thickness didn't risk eye strain.

As far as we are aware, '60 was the first class the Administration invited to make proposals for school improvement before its senior year started.[3] Its representatives addressed this length of study matter and the Administration changed things so that underclass could study to 2300.

The limitations on hours of study have changed as dramatically as the academic regimen. We'll look at that and other changes in 2020's daily life in Bancroft. But before we tell you about daily life in Bancroft nowadays, it's best if we describe the changes on the academic side of campus since those changes explain a lot of the changes in Mother B.

---

2. On a rare occasion the truly desperate could, in later hours, take the disciplinary risk of being out in the corridor, lying prone under one of the dim corridor lights, continuing to try to grasp the concept that was baffling them.

3. The Regs now contain a form for individual Mid's suggestions and a process by which they are forwarded through the Brigade's Midshipman staff to the Administration.

ACADEMICS, THEN

1960 WAS THE LAST CLASS WITH VIRTUALLY NO CHOICE IN WHAT COURSES its members could take. Everyone took the same. Each classroom got the same whether Professor Smith or Lieutenant Jones presided. '60 Mids were given their class-by-class homework assignments for the entire semester, the same as everybody else's, on the first day of class. There were no graded electives. They could not and did not have a "major" or even a "minor."

Perhaps that overstates the uniformity, but only slightly. For language class a Mid could pick his language from among 6: German, French, Spanish, Portuguese, Italian, or Russian. He could choose to try to test into an advanced language class in most, if not all, of those languages. And in some other classes he might be assigned to, not choose, an advanced class. Economics was an example. Being in an advanced class meant he got a top professor and a better textbook.

To get to class, if '60 Mids were to go from Bancroft to the academic complex, or a gym class for that matter, they marched in sections of 15. And though it was a bit more free form if he had a class immediately following, whatever class it was from which he was to return to Bancroft, he marched from it. The commands to the section to go, stop, or turn and the proper conduct of the section were the responsibility of whoever had the duty; it rotated through the section, changing at the start of every week.

The faculty was about fifty-fifty professional academics and commissioned officers.

The professional academics were generally quite good. Many had come to USNA in the '40s when its pay and benefits were far better than anything available elsewhere. That had changed, and some regretted the chains of their retirement package, but pensions in those days before the Employee Retirement Income Security Act (1974) were anti-career-change anchors that didn't vest until taken.

The officers on the faculty were usually USNA graduates who had come off their originally obligated tours at sea, in the air, or in Marine ground assignments. Like most company officers back in Bancroft, most were on their first shore duty. Unlike many officers teaching at West Point, none were permanent academics (and there, in those days, the entire faculty was composed of officers). They were teaching classes but, again like the company officers, probably also trying to pick up a masters at the University of Maryland or, in a few cases, some other D.C./Baltimore area schools. Not to knock them, but in the nature of things the truly academically talented officers approaching their first shore duty were posted to get degrees elsewhere—Harvard, Michigan, Cal Berkeley, MIT, etc.; you get the picture.

The academic departments were headed by Navy Captains working with a top-of-the-department civilian academic. There was no higher civilian academic structure such as existed at other colleges.

To allow for differences in instructor temperament, ability, and grading style, midway through each 16-week semester, instructors were rotated to spare any Mid the class-standing impact of a full semester with the likes of LCDR "2-Oh" Boatman in the front of the room. Remember, 2.5 was the passing grade.

Nevertheless most, but not all, instructors were up to the task. Only one who wasn't comes to mind. The course was chemistry. He was clearly lost at the front of the room. It was routine that when he fumbled, the best student in the room would respectfully ask a question and someone else would suggest an answer, or maybe the star would just ask a "Don't you mean..." question. In either case the point was made to anybody who hadn't picked it up from the homework. About 5 weeks into the term the instructor came to class one day in obvious euphoria. He announced, "I finally got my wish. I'm leaving, going back to what I want to do, fly. I don't know why they had me teach this course, I flunked it when I was here. I wish you guys the best with your new instructor. God bless." He was an exception to be sure, but a memorable one.

'60's Mids attended classes 16 weeks per semester, 5-1/2 days per week. The first semester lasted from Labor Day until the end of January; the second from the end of January to June 1. (Saturday classes were relegated to the dust bin of history in 1989.) 2020's first semester was over by Christmas, the second by mid-May.

'60's Mids were liable to get a quiz at the end of every class. The instructors were required to give a grade on an N-1 basis. That is, if it were a 4 session/week class,

4 was the N. The instructors came to each class armed with a mimeographed quiz. But if they found that it was taking longer for the class to "get it," they could skip the quiz, but only once a week. The quizzes were supposed to take 12-15 minutes, but the more likely scenario was that the instructor often felt the class wasn't getting it and kept teaching until only 6 or, on a good day, 8 minutes were left for the quiz. It seems someone felt that handling the time pressure was as at least as important as knowing the material.

Even though the courses were largely scientific or engineering and the quiz questions admitted of only one right answer, some instructors gave partial credit. That happened when the student obviously knew the principle being taught but perhaps transposed a bit of the data incorrectly before solving the formula of the day. Those indulgent instructors would mark the test CFD (correct for data). Others, like 2-Oh Boatman, an aviator, refused. His point was, "There's no CFD on final approach to a carrier landing."

Daily grades counted for 60% of the course grade, the final exam 40%. Some guys studied hard every day but it never sunk in and they forgot too easily. Some just paid attention in class, stayed well rested, and figured that their gray cells would figure it all out in dream time by the final exam. Others had both talent and energy and they excelled. Different strokes for different folks.

The instructors handed in their lists of grades, probably on Monday morning. The grades were entered into a computer somewhere and—cumulative for the semester to date—were dot matrix-printed and posted on a bulletin board in the battalion areas in Bancroft on Wednesday. A Mid's grade would appear alongside his name as something like 310/9. That meant that his grade total, 3.9 + 3.6 + 2.0 etc., from all his quizzes so far totaled 31.0 after 9 grades. He'd use his slide rule and figure he had a 3.44 to date. It was a semi-private thing. Obviously he could figure out someone else's grade. But mostly that wasn't worth the trouble. Also, as you can see, his grades were on a 4.00 standard, with no As, Bs, or Cs. It was like a grammar school "100% system" on steroids with 4.00 being like 100, 3.96 like a 99, and so forth. Competition was over whisker-like differences.

In 1956-1960 Mids didn't have separate Orders of Merit, or even use the term. Instead, "Aptitude for the Service," a/k/a "Grease," (then a subjective qualitative judgment by one's seniors in his company, the officers in Bancroft, and faculty) was a grade plugged into a Mid's average as if it were an academic course. It was given a greater weight as the years progressed. Nowadays the grading is pretty much the same although your classmates also get to weigh in and the grade is part of one's Military Order of Merit; it does not enter into the Academic Order.

The greatest weight given any academic course went to a research paper '60's Mids had to write in their first class year. And, within that paper, content and presentation counted equally. A Mid might write an excellent paper, but if his typing skills were poor, he kept writing to the last minute, then hired someone from town to type it, and he or she botched it, poor "presentation" would have more effect on his class standing than the grade he earned in a whole year of Calculus.

Yup, the value of appearance was an important lesson at USNA. When you think about it, it was taught every day alongside academic courses. In those days, if a Mid in Bancroft were studying a textbook open on his desk, he was also spit-shining shoes at the near edge of that desk.

The class of '60's curriculum had about 40 courses that included 120 semester hours, comparable to the full load of a contemporary college. It also had 30 semester hours of military content courses such as navigation (piloting and celestial), ordnance & gunnery, etc. Courses that bridged the two worlds, such as Naval Construction and Ship Stability, went into the comparable-to-college category. (What '60's Mids learned in that last one still makes them think about metacentric height while on their couches in 2020 watching *Deadliest Catch*.)

In '60's time Navy taught basic courses—what most colleges would call "101" courses—across a broad range of technical subjects: Chemistry, Physics, Thermodynamics, Fluid Mechanics, Structural Mechanics, Electrical Engineering, Electronics, Aerodynamics, and the like. It also taught basic courses in Economics, History (Europe since 1815, U.S. Diplomatic History, and Naval History) and Literature. Literature included close study of a few books. One of them was *Crime and Punishment*—know your adversary's culture;[1] another was *Pilgrim's Progress*—here's what we want you to know about your culture. See, Religion, *infra*.

These "101" courses did not teach—as majors do—the idea that knowing something in depth is qualitatively different than just knowing the basics. Nor did the school attempt to graduate experts. '60's yearbook, *The Lucky Bag*, characterized the overall curriculum as providing building blocks. Nevertheless, most '60 Mids would now say that the breadth of the offerings served them well in dealing with a wide range of challenges that life in general and Navy life in particular presented. At the very least it enabled them, when dealing with an expert in a field, to know his or her vocabulary and sense when the expert's conclusions didn't ring true.

Still, even the basic course offerings didn't ground the '60 Mids in how to spot and challenge a false argument. Arguably the school didn't want to send officers into the fleet who were schooled in how to disagree. "Commence fire" is not a debate topic. The liberal arts of rhetoric and logic were not on the menu. Neither did USNA teach a basic life-learning lesson of an educated person—don't reject another person's conclusion until you've heard his reasoning. Even in the sciences there was

---

1. All the "-oviches" and "-ovanovas" helped in youngster year recreational reading of Dr. Zhivago.

nothing taught that suggested doubt—no course on probability, no elucidation of the fact that scientific truths are only prevailing theories waiting to be unraveled when they fray at the edges.

The 1956-1960 course selection had one other glaring omission. A Mid in that era could go from being sworn in as a Midshipman on Induction Day to being sworn in as a Commissioned Officer at graduation without ever hearing the phrase "Constitution of the United States" though on those two days it defined what his commitment was all about.[2]

Ethics was a different matter. It wasn't in the curriculum, but it was taught—and well—away from the academic complex and at the other end of Stribling Walk in Bancroft Hall.

In the preface we asked a rhetorical question about what was the essence of a Naval Academy education. Many might say it was extreme, constant, time-limited, competitive pressure. And they'd have cause.

But please permit an author's view. As someone who in the mid-'60s served as a Resident Director of a Freshman "House" in a co-ed dorm at the University of Michigan, I'd say that, if you were looking for the single thing that most made a Naval Academy education different from other quality colleges, it would be that Michigan classrooms were intended for education, dormitories were intended for housing. At Navy both classrooms and the dormitory were there for education. At the U of M a dormitory housing 1100 students employed 45 - 50 grad students. They were mainly there to keep order and secondarily to sense when students needed help and to provide counseling when requested. Except for one Officer of the Watch (OOW), and perhaps an assistant, Bancroft didn't have a paid staff resident at night. Upper classes were there, in charge, and sincerely trying to make each member of a lower class a better future naval officer and a better person. Geographically, Navy education was like a barbell with heavy ends connected by a rod. The connecting rod was Stribling Walk.

Another thing notable about the 1956-1960 course of instruction was the method employed. It was as different from other post-secondary schools as were the course selections. For example, Chemistry was not taught—as it is today in major universities—by a full professor engaged in research giving a Monday lecture to 100+ in a lecture hall and graduate student assistants teaching the other lessons that week to smaller groups while the professor went back to his or her lab. Everything at Navy

---

2. One could conclude that USNA's curriculum in the 1950s was designed to create followers. Followers with leadership skills to be sure, but first of all followers; followers comfortable with defending what is, not worrying about what ought to be. Presumably that was for the civilians to whom the military reported. After all, the 27 stanza poem we were require to memorize (some of us even backwards) ends, "Now these are the Laws of the Navy And many and mighty are they. But the hull and the deck and the keel And the truck of the law is—OBEY".

was taught in small rooms or labs to groups of 15. It followed that what was taught was never cutting edge; it was always long established thought.

And the Navy way of teaching was more direct than Mids imagined teaching was elsewhere.

In an imagined alternate school an instructor in a leadership class might wait for the students to settle down then begin by asking, "Mr. Jones, this class is about leadership, what do you think leadership is?"

At Navy 1956-1960, the instructor, likely a Major or Lieutenant Commander, would briskly enter to an "Attention on Deck," then gesture the at-attention students into their seats but otherwise ignore them, walk to the board and write "Leadership is the art of achieving your goals through the efforts of other people." Then he'd say, "Learn that. It'll be on the test. And note it's not about getting the job done, even perfectly, by doing it yourself. That's fine. But that's not leadership. Now, let's get to the mechanics of it."

Change on the horizon

During the class of 1960's later years at Navy, things were changing or showing signs that they were going to.

In '60's 2/C year the "skinny" (sciences) department introduced an Advanced Science Seminar. It was an invitation-only series of lectures given Friday evenings after dinner. Each lecture featured a guest lecturer, often as not a Nobel Laureate. He gave a broad, but elevated, introduction to his field. Special relativity might be one topic. Light might be another.

What '60's Mids had learned in its normal classes and from the "plebe bible," *Reef Points*, about Professor Michelson was a symptom of the level of our usual instruction. They knew he had been a graduate and then a Professor at USNA and in 1888 had published a paper having something to do with the speed of light. And they knew that he, along with a colleague, had been the first American winners of the Nobel Prize for Physics. And for that they were encouraged to honor him as parochial school kids were urged to venerate a saint.

But his speed of light measurement work had largely been in the 1870s. What made his collaboration with his co-winner and colleague was the Michelson-Morley experiment and its demonstration that the speed of light past a point did not depend on the speed of the point, the speed of the light source, or some "ether" through which the light passed. Only in the Advanced Science Seminar did someone drop that goodie—and go on to talk about how, by 1905, Einstein's thought-experiment-trained mind had hammered that fact into Special Relativity.

In '60's 1/C year the school introduced for-credit electives. They were offered on an overload basis, after normal class hours. They did not count toward '60's averages, a Mid could take no more than 4 overload semester hours per term, and something like 15 additional semester hours were required for a major. *(Jack - Since the overloads gave no grade toward class standing, could not be taken in sufficient numbers to amount to a major, would take time from our other fully demanding studies, etc., I couldn't see how they made sense for our class. Still a friend I respected did take some. Maybe he had a deal to employ credits from an earlier school, maybe he was bored, or maybe, and likely, he was too darn smart [see, the virgin canon caper in the Pranks chapter and Appendix B] to be limited by the reasons that applied to the likes of me. I dunno.)*

One inevitable consequence of the diversity of overloads or other major-validating courses being offered the following year was that marching to class ended the day the class of 1960 graduated.

That's how it was for the class of 1960. But during '60's final years, Admiral Rickover was sounding off with his view that USNA instruction was low quality. The Navy generally didn't groove to Rickover, considering him to be a rude and nasty departure from the Navy way.³ So in the late '50s, the Navy originally wrote off his grumbling about Navy academics as sour grapes.

But something was afoot. After its last exam, and as a complete surprise, '60 was ordered to the Isherwood complex to take the standard, 3-part Graduate Record Exam produced by The Educational Testing Service. If memory serves, the three parts were humanities, history and government, and science. Apparently, somebody wanted to check up on the Admiral's assertions—after all, with his tight personal control over those he selected to serve on his submarines, he was in a position to

---

3. Despite his performance developing nuclear submarines, the Navy had not recommended him for flag rank; Congress gave it to him anyway. There were stories that his time in school was unpleasant and that he was so disliked that his yearbook entry appeared with perforated edges so that it could be removed. That was untrue, though others did receive that treatment.

Some of Rickover's biographers have attributed the Navy's rejection to anti-Semitism. Most of us who had the privilege of a personal interview by him will acknowledge his accomplishments but feel that the Navy's case that he was rude and nasty was spot on. One never knows the true intent of another—especially a selection board—but people who are looking for anti-Semitism in the Navy's attitude toward Rickover are trying to find an inherently unprovable reason where an articulated and demonstrable one exists.

know. '60, as a class, never learned how it did on the GREs.[4]

A couple of years after '60 graduated, Navy shellacked Cornell in an early season football game. A Cornell student wrote a letter published in his alumni news to the effect that Navy Mids were a bunch of knuckle-dragging gorillas. One of Cornell's faculty members, on its Admissions Committee if I recall, wrote a reply published in Cornell's alumni mag and also in Navy's to the effect that Navy may have athletes, but their students also averaged 100 points higher on the SAT verbal aptitude tests than Cornell's. Touché.

Still, that Cornell story only speaks to the ability of USNA students, not their achievement after USNA's instruction.

And at about that same time, in the early '60s, there was also a USNA "academic freedom" issue that made the national magazines. It seems some new civilian Spanish teacher decided to protest a directive that he grade on a curve conforming to the grades given by all other members of the department. His view, as reported, seemed to be that he felt his marching orders meant he should give 3.2s to students that, elsewhere, he would have flunked. He enlisted the aid of the American Association of University Professors on the issue. The press gave the impression that the Superintendent's view was that USNA grades were meant to rank students among USNA peers, not the universe. The Professor would not back down. He was fired.

Over the years there had been some discussion of creating the post of an Academic Dean. But the Navy is a place where the maxim, "If it ain't broke, don't fix it" is honored. With the same inability to identify when things were "broke" that Professor Gelfand detailed in his book *Sea Change at Annapolis* in connection with admission of African-Americans, the admission of women, and the ending of mandatory chapel, successive Superintendents had resisted creating the post of a Dean. If asked, they would have said that an independent authority would lessen their control and, ultimately, the school's military focus. It took someone else to tell USNA its academic system was broke. In 1963 the Secretary of the Navy ordered the

---

4. *(Jack – We were informed how we did individually. I did OK but I was surprised to see that my lowest percentile score was in science. I knew F=MA, even when stated in proper calculus format. What else did anyone need to know? What I didn't know was what planet was 6th from the sun. I was willing to bet that the test was made up by Ivy League liberal arts types who couldn't come close to any of us if they had to use those planets and the stars to find where they were in a trackless ocean. And they probably didn't know entropy from enthalpy, the function of a triode, or vector analysis of a beam load either. But maybe the test showed something more that my instinct to defensive scorn couldn't dismiss. We, the authors, are sure someone took the class' GRE results, normalized them for entering SAT score comparison, and ranked them against schools with SAT-comparable populations and prepared a report for the powers that were. Despite the very able assistance of Dr. Bryan, the Archivist at the Nimitz Library, and with the National Archives closed for the pandemic, we haven't found that report.)*

creation of the post.

Then, in 1966, the Middle States association of Colleges and Secondary Schools arrived for its decennial accreditation visit. It threatened to flunk USNA particularly faulting the plans to merely renovate the library in Mahan Hall. It insisted on the construction of a library capable of accommodating 650 readers. With a master plan for new buildings in place and construction costs for Michelson and Chauvenet already in the budget that demand was unwelcome, but accreditation was vital, so USNA agreed—thus the Nimitz Library.

We don't know how these diverse criticisms, attitudes, surprise exams and such led to curriculum changes. But changes came.

ACADEMICS, NOW

ABOUT THE ONLY THING RECOGNIZABLE TO AN OLD GRAD IS THE FACT that Mids nowadays get the whole semester's homework assignments on the first day of each course

Now there are majors and they define most aspects of a '20 Mid's academic experience. They define his or her (H/H) department, many of H/H faculty, H/H workload, and ultimately H/H earned degree.

The majors are organized into 3 groups: Group I, Engineering; Group II, Sciences; and, Group III, Humanities. USNA is required to graduate a minimum of 80% Group I majors and has never had an issue meeting this requirement. All Humanities majors are required to take several semesters of a language of their choice, some as a major, but most are for a minor. Non-Humanities majors will sometimes take a language to fill a Humanities requirement but most have full schedules and don't.

At the beginning of plebe year every student is assigned an academic advisor who will act as a guide through plebe academics. After a plebe declares a major in March of that year, the advisor is changed to a professor who teaches within that department who will advise that student over the remaining three years. Typically each faculty advisor is responsible for several students but the number varies significantly based on the student/faculty ratio in each department.

The advisor meets with the Mid once a semester to help design the classes to be taken consistent with the requirements of each major, giving consideration to the student's possible previous validation of core courses, summer school classes, graduate education, and research. The result of that meeting is a course matrix. The matrix is fairly standard for plebes since they don't declare their major until March. True, there can be some variation, particularly for plebes who have passed validation tests of early plebe summer. They can get a head start on 3/C courses to fill their schedule and reduce required credits for subsequent years.

As for the class day itself, classes begin at 0755 with "attention on deck" being called by the class leader. The class leader is determined on the first day of school by either volunteer or more often than not, random selection from the attendance list. Each professor runs H/H class slightly differently, some preferring not to call attention, some preferring to take attendance themselves, and some delegating to the section leader. After the roll call, there is very little observed military custom, other than the obvious respect for the professor, since the purpose is first and foremost to create a suitable environment for learning.

Classes are 50 minutes long with ten minutes for transitioning between classes. This is usually plenty of time except when one has a swimming class in Lejeune Hall, by Gate 1, followed immediately by a class on the second deck of Rickover Hall. The students have some freedom to design their preferred schedule and if luck is on their side, they can arrange a free period after phys-ed classes. That is not always a possibility, but professors often make case-by-case exceptions for tardiness by students with unavoidably long treks across the yard.

USNA awards Bachelor of Science degrees to all of its graduates so all Mids are required to take certain core science, technology, engineering, and math (STEM) classes. They include thermodynamics, electrical engineering, calculus, and weapons. Since some of the same topics are very pertinent to engineering majors, there exist different levels of these core classes—e.g., "Engineering Thermo" or "Double Hard Electrical Engineering." There are required physical education classes including swimming, boxing, wrestling, martial arts I and II (perhaps the successors to '60's self-defense course commonly called "hand to gland"[1]), and personal conditioning. For first class year the options are less traditional: e.g., kayaking, golf, rock climbing, and weight lifting.

A typical Engineering major is graded in nearly 50 courses over 4 years. They might include:

Plebe year:
Cyber Security, Calculus, Chemistry, Rhetoric and Intro to Literature, U.S Government and Constitutional Development,[2]

---

1. That on-the-street self-defense course was so described because most techniques taught involved a knee, kick, punch, or Karate chop to the assailant's genitals.
2. Note: both Rhetoric and Constitutional Development. Quite a change!

and American Naval History;

Youngster year:

Physics, Calculus with Vector Fields, Basic Navigation, The West in the Pre-Modern World, Intro to Mechanical Engineering, Ethics and Moral Reasoning, The West in the Modern World, and Strength of Materials;

Second Class Year:

Advanced Navigation, Naval Weapons Systems, Introduction to Design, Engineering Thermodynamics, Materials Science, Electrical Engineering, Mechanical Engineering Experimentation, Applied Thermo, Applications of Cyber Engineering: and,

First Class Year:

Steering the Naval Service through Ethical Shoals, History of the Middle East, Interdisciplinary Capstone Design, Intro to Control Engineering, Energy (Analysis, Policy, and Security), Project Management.

There are grades for Conduct and Aptitude. Conduct is simply a function of demerits; we have already mentioned Aptitude in the previous Daily Life chapter.

Amid all this about academics, we haven't yet touched on how, if at all, the classes of 1960 and 2020 differed when a Mid failed a course.

For the class of 1960 a failing grade in any course meant an appearance before the Academic Board. Its members had three choices: separation; grant of permission to take a re-exam; or, "rolling" the Mid out of his current class back to a succeeding one. A roll back meant that, for example, a Class of '60 Mid might be given the choice of withdrawing from the school or becoming a member of the Class of 1961 or even 1962.

Usually the Board offered a re-exam. About the only times when it didn't were when the Mid's performance on his daily grades or his end-of-semester exam were abysmal or—it was said—when the Mid's Aptitude for the Service ("Grease") grade was so low, or his demerit total so high, as to suggest to the Board that the Navy was better off quit of him. If the Mid's performance on a re-exam proved inadequate, it was back before the Board where the only options remaining were separation or an offer of a rollback.

For the class of 2020 things were different.

If a '20 Mid flunked a course (i.e., earned an "F") there was no re-exam. He or she (H/S) could continue forward. But H/S would be assigned Mandatory Summer School (MSS) addressing the subject failed. It would take the place of one of the two "blocks," other than leave, normally a part of the next summer's experience. If H/S had two "F"s, that meant two blocks of summer school, one of which would take the place of the usual 30-day leave. If H/S earned 2 "D"s H/S would have passed the course and not have to do anything remedial, but H/S would be on academic restriction the next semester, the consequence of which was the loss of specific leave and liberty. Rolling back was still an option in the case of a failed course, but it meant something different than in '60's era. It meant that the failing student would remain in his or her same class, but have to take the flunked course(s) over when next available, often the following year when it was scheduled for the following class. In the case of course failure in 1/C year rolling back or mandatory summer school could prevent a May graduation. The Regs now provide for December graduations, where necessary.

To sum up, the Class of 1960 left Annapolis in the middle of national attention to an open question: What was the quality of USNA academics? Changes were on the horizon, even though resisted by a goodly part of the school's Administration. Those changes came. The result, as of 2020, is that USNA is recognized by *U. S. News & World Report* as the #1 public school, #4 undergraduate engineering program, and #17 among the top all liberal arts colleges in the nation. The school's current Administration and the student body work hard, very hard, to keep and improve those rankings.

7
DAILY LIFE IN BANCROFT, NOW

SO HAS THAT EFFORT AT IMPROVED ACADEMIC STANDING AND STUDENT accomplishment had any effect in Bancroft? Has Mother B's character formation component of the USNA experience diminished? This chapter will address those questions. But to cut to the chase:

Q. Have the changes had any effect in Bancroft?
A. A lot;

Q. Has Bancroft's character formation role diminished?
A. Not on your life.

In '60's time upperclass attention to molding plebes in Bancroft was largely a function of the room and personal inspections, questioning and guidance by upperclass at meals, and disciplinary "come arounds" by such upperclass as took the trouble to conduct them. Those who took the trouble did so out of concern for the plebes' development, but that effort was not mandatory and a bother. As a result the overall effort was uneven. There was even a well-recognized difference in the severity of the plebe experience from one Battalion to another.

To tell the story of how it is now, let's start with '20's waking-up rituals.

For many the typical day begins with morning workouts at 0530. Plebes muster with their Company Training Staff. Those in any class in danger of flunking the Physical Readiness Test muster with the Company Physical Mission Staff. And varsity athletes muster with their teams. Those who fit none of these categories enjoy an extra hour of sleep to 0630. The workout groups are typically back on deck by 0630, in time to hear the same damn bell as '60 heard. But nowadays the bell sounds only the long blast, the shorts are gone. The obligation to get up is still in the Regs but generally not enforced—certainly not with honor code consequences. The only actually constraining requirement is to be dressed and presentable in time to make Morning Quarters formation at 0700. It is followed by a cafeteria (a/k/a rolling tray) service, random seating breakfast—if desired.

There is now no requirement to remove all the bedding from its tucked under state. In fact, except for plebe summer, '20's requirements for bed appearance are generally a notch below '60's. The beds are now in a wood furniture bed-above-desk combination that could not be as easily moved from the bulkhead as the pipe formed racks of '60's day.

Making the bed properly requires taking the mattress down, making it, and boosting it back, made, onto its elevated place. As a consequence, during the academic year virtually no one in '20 slept under their sheets. The norm is to use one's blanket for cover but sleep on top of the made bed. The tight military tucks and hospital corners on the made beds are semi-permanent, held in place with all manner of fixes known to man: safety pins, shirt holders, even duct tape. (Some truths never change.[1] Both classes learned one of life's essential lessons, "If it moves, but it shouldn't: duct tape; if it should move, but it doesn't: WD-40.")

"Come arounds," now explicitly reserved for preparing plebes for their weekly professional knowledge test on Friday evenings, are still authorized, but, at least in the Regs, only for 20 minutes from 0635 to 0655. Given that upperclass are either showering after their workout or still sleeping, come arounds are more often held in the afternoon or evening. It is the plebes' responsibility to arrange a time with the upper class.

Come arounds are now a series of three meetings during the week, first with the plebes' assigned 3/C mentors, then their 2/C fire team leaders, and then with their 1/C squad leaders. The purpose of the come arounds is to quiz the plebes on their knowledge of the professional topic of the week, about which they take a written test Friday evening. These topics included ship and aircraft identification, marine weapons, aviation history, foreign affairs, special warfare community history, and other such relevant Navy topics. A Mid could fail these tests at the company standard (92%), battalion standard (80%), or brigade standard (70%). A failure at any of these levels would result in increasing levels of upperclass attention, including additional come arounds with midshipmen Training Staff at the battalion or brigade level.

After the 0700 formation, and breakfast if taken, Mids proceed individually, or in whatever social grouping they choose, to their first period (0755) classrooms.

Noon meal formation is held at 1205 if outdoors and 1200 if indoors. Noon meal is the only mandatory, prescribed-seating meal of the day. All are released at 1235 and have about an hour before the afternoon classes resume at 1330.

The 1545 to 1800 time slot is the Athletic Reserve Period. Varsity teams practice in that time and all others participate in intramural competition if they have a game on that day. Typically each intramural team participates in two games per week. Holding a practice is unheard of. Intramural warriors are the quintessential Non Athletic Regular Persons. Seasonal exceptions to intramurals are allowed for some, often competitive, activities—debate team practice or Glee Club rehearsal, for example.

NARPs who do not have a game that day are left to their own devices for a

---

1. There has been a similar change in the haircut aspect of weekly life. Haircut standards are considerably relaxed. Bancroft now has only one barber shop, the one in the First Wing. There is no pressure or in-company process for appointments though a Mid can call the shop and get one. Most haircuts are done on a walk-in basis. Once a month is often more than enough to avoid a failed inspection. And that's for males. Most of the women avoid the barbershop altogether; the haircuts they received on I-day are reason enough. They make other arrangements, often in town.

personal workout at one of the gyms, calisthenics on the athletic fields, or a run. Perhaps the most coveted afternoon personal workout is an off-the-yard run. Running routes are defined in the regs (one is pictured below in the chapter on Liberty and Leave) and may be used at any time, not otherwise scheduled, from sunrise to sunset. They are explicitly required to be for running or jogging but not walking or bike-riding. Runners and joggers are not authorized to stop anywhere, save only for required bathroom use at perhaps a McDonald's or a gas station. This escape from the yard on a weekday allows mids to get away from the stresses of daily life for a while. Plebes are no exception to these runs which are arguably the most freedom they ever enjoy during the day.

Mandatory dinner was eliminated shortly before '20 arrived on campus. Dinner is now served, cafeteria style ("rolling tray") with random seating, from 1730 to 1930. The uniform for the meal is "Blue and Golds or better." "Blue and Golds" is a comfortable track suit uniform, and as such, company training staffs often revoke permission to wear it for plebes.

Extracurricular Activities usually meet from 1900 to the start of the study period at 2000. This, as in days of antiquity, has unofficially become the most popular time for plebe come arounds.

The study period lasts, formally, until 2200. It is a sacred time reserved for academic study only. Informally, studying lasts beyond that. Plebes are supposed to be in bed by 2300 but they can request, get from their squad leader, and post on their door a permission slip (a/k/a "late lights chit") to study past 2300. The permission slip process allows the squad leaders to track their plebes' time management so that the plebes could be counseled if things get out of hand.[2]

Members of all other classes may study as late as they like. This is a significant problem for many students due to the academic rigors of the curriculum. Sleep deprivation is rampant. In the core time of the tougher terms, 5 hours sleep a night is a common average. While coffee is served in King Hall during morning and noon meals, energy drinks are exceedingly popular. It is not uncommon to see caffeine in the forms of Monster, Xyience, Red Bull, coffee, Rockstar, KickStart, etc., during class and even well into evening study hours.

Back in '60's day significant attention was paid to the development of plebes and to a lesser extent, others in Bancroft. Nowadays that has been more than 'kicked up a notch.' We've already mentioned Company Training Staffs, Company Physical Mission Staffs, and Squad Leader responsibilities for plebe sleep/study hours.

---

2. As a consequence of plebes being able to study late, they are now allowed, by the Regs, back in their racks during the day when not required to be at a class or lunch or during afternoon athletic or evening study time. But company training staffs often reinstate the nap ban in their company.

Companies also have a Mid academic officer who organizes study groups, assigns tutors to struggling midshipmen, and tracks academic progress on all Mids in the company.

But there's more than that. Each company has an assigned Senior Enlisted Leader (SEL) with an office next to the Company Officer's. These men and women hold the ranks of Chief (E-7) or Senior Chief Petty Officer (E-8) in the Navy, or Staff Sergeant (E-6), Gunnery Sergeant (E-7), or Master Sergeant (E-8) in the Marine Corps. They assist the Company Officer and prepare the Mids for their future in which they will have to develop relationships with their senior enlisted men and women, balancing having seniority over them while learning from their significant professional experience.

For the needs of Mids going through hard times each Battalion has an assigned Chaplain who is prepared to offer religious or non-religious counseling. Chaplains offer total confidentiality and will not report on matters discussed so that Mids have the freedom to speak their concerns without fear of adverse consequences. The only exception to this rule is if the Chaplain believes that a Mid is in danger of hurting him/herself or others.

In addition to this resource, '20's Mids also have access to the Midshipmen Development Center (MDC) which is staffed with licensed counselors and psychiatrists. Mids are authorized and encouraged to seek professional help for their mental health at any point during their four years at the academy.

Each company has a wardroom which functions as a social space for the upper class and a meeting place for company training. The wardrooms are managed by the 1/C Wardroom Officer. In most cases the wardroom contains a full store of snack food for purchase, a large TV that is usually playing some sporting event but also is used for video gaming and movie nights. There is also an assortment of couches and chairs for lounging. Companies usually finance a WIFI connection,[3] speaker system, fridge, microwave, and other such conveniences with dues paid at the start of each semester.

The existence of the wardroom parallels the fleet concept of a space for officers only. While Mids display very little etiquette in the company wardroom, it is at least a place that plebes are not authorized to be without permission and therefore a place where seniors can chill with colleagues away from the judging eyes of subordinates.

As you probably have gauged by now, the attention to the development of plebes in Bancroft is more conscious and focused than ever. Going along with that there is a governing idea that every upperclass Mid's development should include

---

3. At the end of 2020's time the Facilities staff installed 5G WIFI throughout Bancroft. But the company wardrooms still purchase their own for WIFI games and other applications not supported by the new standard system.

experience in leadership and its responsibilities. Implementation of that idea is even far more extensive than we have intimated to this point.

Consider the following list of assignments in a typical company:

Company 1/C billets

Company military Chain of Command (COC) in descending order
Company Commander
Company Executive Officer (XO)
Company Sergeant major – highest 2/C billet in company
4 platoon commanders
12 squad leaders – some are 2/C
24 fire team leaders (2 per squad) – mostly 2/C
All 3/C are assigned a plebe or two as mentees

Logistical 1/C billets – in no particular order
Training officer
Physical mission officer (PMO)
Wardroom officer
Academics officer
Public affairs officer (PAO)
Operations officer
Safety officer
ADEO (alcohol and drug education officer)
SAPR guide (Sexual Assault Prevention and Response) – sometimes 2/C
SHAPE guide (Sexual Harassment and Assault Prevention Education) – sometimes 2/C
Adjutant
Admin officer
1st Lieutenant
Drill officer

Each of these billet holders, once appointed, then "hires" a 3/C and a 2/C to assist. In this manner, everyone in company usually has some sort of responsibility for running a part of the company and is a part of their Staff Chain of Command (COC) as well as their Military COC.

Rob - This can get a little bit confusing especially for someone in my position as a 1/C. I was at the top of the Staff Chain of Command as the Brigade First Lieutenant and wore 4 stripes for that billet. My military COC was still in the company, so I reported to my 2/C squad leader and then to my platoon commander who wore only two stripes and thus appeared to be the junior in our relationship, etc.

In a way, this system mimics the fleet quite well since we will belong to different COCs simultaneously, e.g., ship type commands such as Cruiser/Destroyer Force Atlantic, and operational commands such as Second Fleet.

Midshipmen still stand watches in Bancroft. The main function of the '60-era watchstander was communication. For '20, that's still a watchstander's principal function, but communications have come a long way.

The company-level watchstander of today still has a post with a land line that will occasionally distribute calls from the Main Office. The entire watch standing structure from the top (the Officer of the Watch) down to the company–level is connected through personal cell phones. Alternative to texting and calling, the daily watch standers at the Brigade, Regimental, and Battalion level rely on apps such as a GroupMe to quickly communicate up and down the chain while keeping everyone in the loop.

The academy runs on email. As a millennial, it is hard to imagine a world without the internet; it is also hard to imagine the Academy without email. The average midshipmen will receive anywhere from 20-40 emails per day. Midshipmen who climb the ranks to staff or commander roles will up that number to nearly 100. Many of the emails are midshipmen ads to "join this club" or "come and watch this performance." Those get deleted first. Then there are emails from the business division: "don't forget to bring your worn uniforms to the tailor shop," "the barber shop will not be open on Tuesday," or "the Mid store is now selling new T-shirts." Finally, there are the important emails, ones concerning watch standing, billet related info, and communications from the academic domain at the other end of Stribling. It is expected that Midshipmen check their email multiple times a day; most just link their emails to their phones. It is not explicitly a rule that a Mid own a smart phone; however, it is an expectation that the chain of command can get in contact with a Mid at just about any time. It amounts to the same thing.

Texting can be used for formal communication; even between plebes and upper classmen if the upper classman has already consented to its use. Texting is used frequently to communicate excusals from formation, reminders for watch, and of course constant social interaction.

The Academy is now a very connected digital world. From email to group messaging apps, social media, phones, and texting, the lines of communication are extremely fast. Some things don't change though; as '60 learned the first day: "There's always 2% that don't get the word." Time and time again frustration reigns when someone "didn't read their email" or "never saw that text;" watches are still missed, excusals are still unaccounted for, and Mids still get fried.

Social Media at the Academy.

No discussion of change at the Naval Academy from 1956 to 2020 can ignore the simple fact of social media. It may be a blessing or a curse—and there are those who see it simplistically as one or the other. We will make no attempt to judge the net of its positive and negative effects. Rather, we will give you some sense of the kinds of undeniable change these media have brought to the people affected by the goings on at the Academy.

Inside the walls, Midshipmen find themselves a part of many different groups: companies, teams, clubs, watch sections, and academic study groups. It is routine that during the formation of any group, all get out their phones and add their names to the group's chatroom on an app such as GroupMe. The tone on the group chats can vary from professional to social but ultimately the chats are an excellent tool for keeping everyone informed—even about rumors.

Also, for Midshipmen, social media have drastically improved communication with family and friends off of the yard, increased virtual social interaction, and created the means to share and receive pictures, videos, and posts about their lives. In some ways this may have made the lives of midshipmen harder. Now, young men and women, whose earlier thoughts of the Naval Academy focused on what they are gaining by going to an Academy, are able to see how the lives of their friends at regular colleges compare. Now they can see what they are missing.

It also needs to be said that, while starting at the academy is a trying experience for incoming plebes, it is also a trying experience for their parents. Hovering parents who, in an earlier time had to simply grin and bear what they learned in a bi-weekly phone call or an occasional letter, are now enabled by social media as never before. They have more insight into their child's experience at USNA. Facebook pages such as "BLB" (Blind Leading the Blind) have sprung up as a means for parents of Mids to get in touch with other Mid parents to ask questions about the USNA process and discuss current events at the Academy. It is also a breeding ground for rumors and gossip. This ability for parents to communicate freely has contributed somewhat to a "helicopter parent" culture that is seriously unpopular with Midshipmen who are just trying to get away from home and grow up.

The impulse toward self-expression has always been a challenge for people in uniform. Traditionally Midshipmen have expressed their creativity and humor in the form of pranks. In addition to the creation and circulation of in-house memes, social media have brought a new form of covert self-expression. Apps such as Facebook, Instagram, and Tumblr have enabled midshipmen to open anonymous accounts under names like "Navy Barstool," "Mylifeismid," "Unsat," and "Nimitzcoffeebar." Other apps including Yik-Yak, Jodel, and Twitter enable midshipmen to anonymously post chats that anyone with an account can view and reply to. These chats offer the administration an insight into the general feeling of the Brigade. More importantly they are visible to the general public and that has presented serious issues for the school's administration.

Yet, in some ways, social media has become a valuable means for the leadership to reach the Brigade, and not just at the get-out-the-word level. At a more casual level during the unprecedented events of COVID-19, the Commandant created daily messages of encouragement and posted them on Instagram during the long absence of Midshipmen from the yard. The postings were styled as the *Dant Daily*.

All in all, social media have had a profound effect on the culture at USNA. In 2020 the full spectrum of the social media universe is a central part of socialization between Mids and their contacts with the rest of the world. It has opened doors for far-reaching self-expression that never entered the minds of the class of '60. For the administration, social media has been both a nightmare and a highly useful tool. Whatever the net of the pluses and minuses, it is current reality.

8
YOUNGSTER CRUISE

After the end of its first academic year, '60 went to sea on its first cruise. It started on the afternoon of the class of 1957's graduation in the new Halsey Field House. Members of the class of '60 went from there directly to the Herdon Monument for the climb that would confirm their liberation from the status as lowly plebes. What members of later classes will note from the picture is that in 1960, because of the timing, the climb was attempted in dress whites with the tunic removed.

More about that tradition later.

After a quick change of uniforms, '60 Mids left for their cruise, some by launch to ships anchored in the bay.

Others were transported to Norfolk by LSTs (Landing Ship, Tank) and joined the ships they were to cruise on there

In Norfolk the USNA Mids were joined by Naval Reserve Officer Training Corps (NROTC) Mids from across the nation. The ships stayed in Norfolk a few days for an international naval review by the Queen of England celebrating the 350th anniversary of the Jamestown Colony. (She has since reprised her gig for the 400th.) The most memorable part of all that was not standing like potted plants at the ships' rails watching royalty as she stood at the rail of one of her Navy's cruisers, waving like she was screwing in a light bulb. It was pulling liberty in a town filled with 40,000 sailors from most of the free world's navies.

Starting in Norfolk and on the cruise in general, '60 performed in the roles of enlisted men—shining instantly re-tarnishing brass, teaming up like chain gangs to holystone a cruiser's or battleship's teak deck,[1] standing watches as lookouts, as engine room gofers taking hourly readings of bearing temperatures between paint or sweeping chores, and as boiler room firemen throttling feed water into the what were, in essence, room-sized furnace-kettle combinations.

The Mids slept in 4-bunk-high tiers, "triced up" when empty, in rooms that were standard enlisted quarters but were occupied only by Mids. The commodes in the heads of the larger ships were beyond crude. They had the same design as a long horse trough in an old western movie, 6 pairs of slats served as toilet seats. The seawater flush entered at the high end and carried excrement and, reportedly, occasionally some joker's blazing island of toilet paper, under the rumps downstream to the drain. Privacy for such times was only possible if one could wait until getting off the mid-watch shortly before 4 a.m. (*The three photos above are from yearbooks, The Lucky Bag, 1960, 1960, and 1958 respectively.*)

From Norfolk the ships headed south. Some other exclusively NROTC-

---

1. Holystoning was an evolution in which a hard rough object, usually a rough brick such as the kind used to line a ship's boiler, a firebrick, was rubbed across a wetted and sanded wooden deck to smooth it. Routinely the brick had a depression in it into which a broom handle was inserted so the guy at the other end of the handle could move the brick back and forth while standing. In practice the guy doing the rubbing did it in a chain gang-like line of others similarly tasked, usually singing work songs to set the rhythm of the action and to ease the monotony. As for why major combatants had teak decks in the middle of the 20th century, you'll have to ask somebody else.

carrying vessels, including the USS Wisconsin, steamed along for a couple of days, then split off to transit the canal and hit ports on South America's west coast. *(Jack – In the summer 2019 I ran into a man who had been a 3/C NROTC Mid on that cruise.[2] Over beers and watching dusk overtake the Teton Mountains we swapped stories; his included the report that the sailors on their ships told the local lovelies in various ports that the guys with the blue rings on their hats had VD.)* The rest of us not transiting the canal steamed directly south, crossed the equator with the usual Navy grabass (that is, humbling stuff that would not be imposed on paying passengers crossing the line on a civilian cruise ship), and steamed on to Brazil.

Before we go on about our complete itinerary we should mention that, among other things we learned while steaming south (though we had never doubted) was that the Navy is a dangerous business. One day a cruiser, *USS Canberra*, came up one sailor short at morning quarters. He was never found and was presumed to have gone overboard intentionally, accidentally, or otherwise during the night. At another point on another cruiser, a couple of Marines relieving their watch over special weapons had a quick draw contest, a sidearm discharged, a Marine lost a lung. His ship went flank (for civilian readers, that's the notch above full speed) to get him to a Brazilian port half a day early.

Later in the cruise there was another incident born of boredom during a waiting period in a gunnery exercise on a destroyer. The gun captain elevated the barrels of the guns in his mount. That depressed the breech (loading) ends where one severed the misplaced leg of an inattentive resting gunner.

The primary destination of our cruise was Brazil. The description of those ports of call will come in a bit. But first back to the ships' itinerary.

The ships' planned itinerary included, after Brazil, a port visit to Guantanamo. But while the cruise was at sea, some revolutionaries active in the adjacent *Oriente* province seized—"kidnapped," the press reported—a busload of Navy sailors returning from liberty in the nearby town of Caiminera. Their leader, Fidel Castro, thought better of it and the matter was resolved reasonably quickly. But the gate connecting the base and civilian Cuba was closed. Our visit was cancelled. The gate remains closed today.

So instead, after Brazil, the ships headed to different ports. Unlike Gitmo none was large enough for the entire fleet. Some ships went to San Juan, others to Trinidad (then in the British West Indies), and the rest to St. Thomas in the U. S. Virgin Islands. For those slotted into San Juan that meant USDA-approved milk, not the powdered stuff they had been drinking for a month and a half; the Caribe Hilton with its gaming rooms and swim-up bar; and, the Reserve Officers' Club where the

---

2. He had gone on to graduate from Georgia Tech and had made a good living as an engineer. (Also I asked, and he admitted that he, like me, never used calculus after he left school.)

10th Naval District Steel Drum Band played uncommonly mellow music.[3]

Then ships from our cruise and ships that had earlier transited the canal formed up for a naval gunfire exercise at Culebra. It was probably the last time two Iowa-class battleships fired in line together. Their guns' noise was unremarkable; not so the feeling of each shot's pressure wave, even on the deck of a ship a thousand yards away. During that firing exercise somewhere in each of the task force's ships, '60 Mids played every conceivable enlisted role needed to send ordnance down range. *(Jack – I fed bags of gunpowder into the breech of one of a cruiser's 8-inch guns.)*

After the shoot it was north and up the Bay to Crabtown where, though '60 had been 3/C since '57 had graduated in June, and not plebes since the successful Herndon climb, by tradition its members became youngsters upon sighting the chapel dome.

Now, about '60's visit to Brazil.

Most of the ships went to Rio. Some *(Jack - including mine, the cruiser* USS Macon*) went to Santos. Santos was the world's largest coffee port but it was also a poverty-ridden, rainy, could-be-anywhere, unremarkable port town.)*

Fortunately, the Navy had stuff planned for the Santos Mids in the then-burgeoning but small and charming Sao Paulo. It was a city filled with beautiful and energetic people. It lay 45 miles inland from Santos, up the escarpment. Buses took the Mids from Santos up a dramatically engineered switch-back-rich highway.

A few years earlier Brazil had no domestic auto industry. It had been bleeding currency purchasing foreign cars, so it had banned their importation. Volkswagen was quick to respond and had just opened a plant in Sao Paulo's outskirts. With that the city became where industry was happening in Brazil. In 2020 it has a population of over 11 million in the city proper, 22 million in the Metro Area, and 43 million in the same-named state.

But the Navy had done more than give the Mids whose ships had docked in Santos a peek at Sao Paulo. It had arranged an opportunity to buy a tour package of a bus ride and a first class hotel in Rio for 4 days. (It seems nobody thought to give the guys who anchored in Rio the opportunity to pay for a 300-mile bus ride to a hotel in Santos.) Of course Rio was beautiful, but just as obviously it was not as industrially energetic as Sao Paulo. Apart from the poverty of its large hill-side shanty town, its favela, it was avowedly a tourist and party town—Copacabana Beach, the Carioca spirit, and all that jazz, don'ja know. That (along with the hope to open up inland parts of the country) was a significant reason the nation started to build a new capital city, Brasilia, in 1957 and moved its government there in 1960.

---

3. Colloquially referred to as "Admiral Dan's Shit Can Band." Admiral Dan Gallery, then the Commandant of the 10th Naval District, had been Captain of the *USS Guadalcanal* on 6/4/44 when it captured the *U-505*, the flag of which is in Memorial Hall.

Chapter 8 - Youngster Cruise

Those Mids who were taking Portuguese, or could force their Spanish to serve, read in the local newspapers about a reportedly important upcoming sporting event. In those days long before ESPN, if we had been state-side we wouldn't have known of it. But in various ways some of us got tickets and went on Sunday to the 200,000-seat Maracanã Stadium to see our first big-time soccer game. It was Argentina v. Brazil. The locals lost, 2-1 but they remember it for the first "cap" and the first international goal by some kid a year and a half younger than the youngest member of '60. It was, of course, Pelé. He led them to a World Cup victory the following year (and in 2 of the 3 World Cups after that, failing only when a cheap shot blew out his knee and sidelined him in an earlier round).

Reasonable inquiry also led Mids to recommendations to a view of the City from the walkway around the base of the Christ the Redeemer statue at the top of Corcovado. The idea was to be there at dusk and watch the lights of the city come on. (*Photo below from 1958 Lucky Bag*)

Jack - I was on the from-Santos tour. After the game I met up with my hotel roommate and went to Corcovado. It's a very long stone stair climb to the top. We skipped an elevator that, for a small charge, could take us most of the way there. When we reached the elevator exit level, another '60 USNA Mid came out of the elevator with a beautiful Brazilian girl and her middle-aged chaperone. Of course, they were en route *to the same view of the city. Surprisingly it wasn't crowded. The five of us watched the city's conversion to night life for the better part of an hour, chatting while we did.*

Then the chaperone, seeing she was cramping a good thing and sensing my roommate and I were tolerable company, turned to us and said, "Let's leave these kids alone." We left for her luxury apartment in the Ipanema section, walking past the well-guarded Brazilian White House on the way. At her place we talked about all manner of stuff including how affluent people preserved their wealth in a country with roaring inflation (diamonds, not banks). Eventually she kicked back her spectacular Persian rugs, poured another round of scotch, and taught us the Samba. A glorious day, not one I could have had stateside on summer break from any ordinary college in those days.

'60's Youngster Cruise was the last of many grand Midshipmen-centered cruises. The next year 3/C were split up most to join a Second Fleet Cruise from Groton, Connecticut to the Iberian Peninsula and back to Norfolk, or a Sixth Fleet cruise in the Med. Thereafter, including for '60's first class cruise, individual Mids were sent to individual ships to join the on-going routine. It should be said though, that year all the 3/C in the class of '62 sailed together with 40 members of '60 on Operation Inland Seas (described later in the Chapter on First Class Summer).

USNA's current plan for what it hopes to achieve by its program for summer training over the three summers after plebe summer is set forth in an instruction. In essence it breaks each summer into three blocks, one of which is, almost always, leave.

Usually one of the blocks for current '20s-era youngster cruises fits the join-an-individual-ship's-on-going routine format. A difference is that while '60's Mids played the role of enlisted sailors yet—except for sharing watches, battle station drills, and work assignments—they generally lived apart from their enlisted counterparts—at least on the larger ships. '20's Mids were paired with an enlisted sailor upon arrival on board and were to be mentored by that sailor. Many of the class of '20 tell stories of memorable experiences like '60 had, at sea and ashore. Your co-author in this project does not, at least on the "at sea" side of things. He was unfortunately assigned to an LPD[4] which wasn't a bad ship but it was in its pre-commissioning phase. As such, it didn't go out for more than one night and he spent the rest of the month working pier-side. However, there was plenty of liberty in San Diego to be had, so he's not complaining.

One of this project's contributors, Josh, was on the same ship as Rob. But, unlike Rob, he had not been in the Navy before USNA. He may have missed out on the experience of being at sea, but he learned a lot. The details of shipboard life were new to him. And he was paired with a sailor who worked in the galley. The long days of preparing for, serving, and cleaning up after 3 meals for a whole crew, with the execution of all the routine but essential tasks involved, was an enlightening, humbling, and respect-generating experience for him.

Another contributor, Rick, likewise drew a short straw. He had a sub cruise lined up. He was looking forward to it as his father, a grad, Class of '88, made a career of subs and had commanded a nuke attack boat. But medical issues intervened and Rick wound up on a surface command.

Yet, due to the 3 blocks concept, '20's youngster summer was also not a one-trick pony as '20's fleet cruise was only one of three blocks, 30 days, not 60. Another

---

4. Landing Platform, Dock—somewhat less descriptive than "Amphibious Transport Dock" by which it is denominated in the register, but somehow it had to start with an "L."

block for most,[5] of course, was leave. The third was professional training. That could mean a whole range of things including Off Shore sailing, a Yard Patrol Craft (YP) Cruise to New England, NOLs,[6] or a detail on campus in support of a summer seminar or STEM class.

For his 3/C "Professional Development" assignment Rob did offshore sailing including Annapolis to Newport, then a race (using celestial navigation) to Bermuda, and finally Bermuda back to Annapolis. In lieu of holystoning he had the experience of sailing with another boat—and because his had a disabled motor—proceeding when becalmed under tow from that other boat whose motor was working.

Josh did the Yard Patrol Craft cruise from Annapolis to Baltimore, Philadelphia, New York, and Boston spending a lot of time navigating (mostly piloting) in restricted or coastal waterways. Ashore he and his classmates had city tours and plenty of roam-around time in American cities often new to them.

Spencer missed the 30-day Youngster Cruise for medical reasons. She took a voluntary summer school course in Navigation and training for the SHAPE (Sexual Harassment and Assault Prevention Education) program, the education program as distinguished from SAPR which is more of a response program. That training prepared her for leading discussion groups her 3/C year. (She progressed with SHAPE training in each of her remaining summers. More about this later.)

Rick's second block was teaching rising high school seniors as a STEM (Science, Technology, Engineering, and Math) detailer and pulling some time as a welcomer, greeting STEM students at the airport, then travelling with them to the campus while

---

5. Notable exceptions were: varsity athletes either in fall sports with NCAA approved training schedules or spring sports with on-going competitions beyond the end of the academic year; and the less academically successful who were assigned two Mandatory Summer School sessions. For such folks there was no summer leave.

6. This was a month with the private adventure firm, National Outdoor Leadership. Such a block was allowed as part of the curriculum but any Mid choosing it had to arrange privately to pay for it. For an example visit tiny.cc/ca8-1 (or scan QR8-1 on page 68).

familiarizing them with Maryland (his home state) and what they would encounter when they got on campus. For third block he gave up his leave for wrestling training.

QR8-1

tiny.cc/ca8-1

9 SECOND CLASS SUMMER

Aviation Summer – Part One

For the Class of 1960 the summer between youngster and second class years was, like Caesar's Gaul and all of 2020's non-plebe summers, divided in three parts.

It was called aviation summer, but that's a caption that didn't tell the whole story—or even refer to a major part, Marine/Amphib Navy exposure. This chapter will detail that. The next chapter will detail 1960's two-part aviation experience and then turn to our 2020 contributors' description of their second class summers.

The day after celebrating the graduation of the Class of '58 (the class that had made '60's plebe lives as "instructive" as it could) the class of '60 found itself in Quonset huts on a piece of Tidewater land south of Virginia Beach and north of the Carolina line. They were meeting often previously unknown classmates as they were assigned to new platoons, not by foreign language groupings, but by alphabet. The purpose of their being in Tidewater was to learn about, and eventually participate in, an amphibious invasion.

The format was simple enough: monotonously repetitive sand table briefings and physical practice. The physical practice involved a lot of running around in the sand while carrying rifles, jumping into helicopters about to take off and out of those which had just landed,[1] and scrambling up and down wooden walls on cargo nets.

The sand-table[2] briefings were as memorable for the Quonset hut discussions

---

1. For many, those helicopter rides, holding on for dear life trying to stay clear of the open side door, were their first time in an airplane.
2. Large-table-size 3-D representations of the subject landscape.

about them as the briefings themselves. They would start with some Marine Officer moving a long pointer over the table identifying features of the land to be invaded. Then "**BANG!**" a cherry bomb hidden in the back of the table would go off. The officer would then explain that at H-hour[3] Minus 5 minutes a "tactical" nuclear bomb would be delivered to obviate the need for a naval gun fire barrage *a la* the WWII invasions, or the 1950 Korean War invasion at Inchon, or the one '60 had participated at Culebra during the summer before.

What the instructor taught after the bang is not memorable. It probably involved stuff '60 had learned in plebe year preparing a response to "professional questions" asked at lunch by a 1/C coming from his Naval History course's session on the British mistakes at Gallipoli: stuff the Vikings knew long ago and the Normans knew a thousand years ago. Stuff like "load your ships so you don't send your equipment ashore before the troops, otherwise when the battle is joined the defenders will have the equipment and your guys will not." As they say nowadays, not rocket science.

Back in the Quonsets, with songs like *Peggy Sue*[4] playing on the radio, Mids had conversations rooted in the not-always-wrong certainty of know-it-all youth. They discussed the military tendency to train for the last war. While the planners of this invasion had helicopters, they weren't using them. No doubt the planners had heard about the invasion of Normandy in 1944, may had even been there, but they hadn't learned its lesson that invasions do not permit committing troops on a 5-minute time line. The Mids knew the planners had heard of the lethality of nuclear weapons but figured the planners hadn't a clue that sending troops into a just-nuked battlefield was likely to involve "un-good" radiation levels that would at least impair those troops' combat abilities. And that was assuming the troops hadn't already died in the blast. After all, at H-hour minus 5 minutes they would have been less than 2,000 yards off the beach in open landing craft even in the unlikely event that the schedule was working perfectly.

Also troubling was the thought that the planners had assumed that the defenders didn't have nukes to use at H-hour PLUS 5 minutes. Years later that consideration brought an after-the-fact shudder to the Class of '60 Mids reflecting on the time they were close to a non-nuclear-assisted invasion of the later-revealed-to-be tactically nuclear armed Cuba in October of 1962. See the movie *Thirteen Days*.

In the nature of their pseudo-combat preparations, '60's Mids wore considerably less-than-parade-grade uniforms. There was a counterpoint, and an

---

3. Standard terminology for the time the first wave of the invasion force hits the beach.

4. Other popular songs of that year such as *Chantilly Lacy* and *La Bamba* weren't released yet. You know where that is headed. If you don't, checkout *American Pie* at tiny.cc/ca9-1 (or scan QR9-1 on page 74).

annoying one at that. The United States Air Force Academy had been formed, but it was a full year from graduating its first class. It sent a large detachment of cadets assigned to the amphib training base to observe what an established Academy did. They observed Mids forming up to march (sort of) to meals, sweating on their way back to their Quonsets at the end of a day playing in sand and mud, and generally performing in purposeful but laid back military fashion. Usually the cadets observed from bleachers, seated there in their designed-by-Cecil B. DeMille sky blue uniforms.

The Mids hoped the cadets could view them as being in a 'get real' mode, but apparently reality was lost on them.

That came to a head when one of them or their accompanying officers put a Mid on report for theft. It seems that in choosing among the practices of its academy forbearers, USAFA had chosen West Point's practice of first call to reveille. So, long before Navy reveille, the loud speaker in the adjacent USAFA Quonset complex blared out "first call"—apparently so they could get up, get formally dressed, and watch the Mids wake up. One evening our hero took a towel from one of the USAFA clothes lines, climbed the telephone pole to the speaker, and stuffed it into silence. Thus the conduct report. Fortunately, the matter was adjudged by naval officers and was dismissed with a comment amounting to the well-known governing legal principle, "The law is not an ass."

We don't know what the Administration of USAFA intended, but they had, and squandered, an opportunity for inter-service bonding and real learning. They would only have had to put their charges in working uniforms, spread them among the Mids, and sent them into helicopters and to sea with their contemporaries from the long established Academy.

Eventually, '60 escaped the judging eyes of their Colorado comrades. They put to sea on amphibious transport ships for three days culminating in an invasion of an undefended Virginia shore.

Jack- Personal note: Each of our memories of the invasion day is no doubt different. But I think mine is representative and the best way to convey something of our various memories; a homogenized abstract telling would not get as near the truth of that day.

I went up on deck at 0300, three hours before our over-the-side time. The sea was fairly calm but at first light a strong breeze was coming up from the south, parallel to the beach. In about an hour there was a considerable and growing swell running before the wind. I was partnered with an alphabetically close, "K"-named classmate I barely knew. (Ironically, when the 7th wing construction connection to the 5th ousted me from my room 1/C year, we became roommates). At 0600 we clambered down the cargo nets into our assigned landing craft. Our training had prepared us for the dangers of boarding a rising and falling landing craft alongside a rolling transport in an elevated sea state. Our boat was a "Mike Boat," an LCM-8 (Landing Craft, Medium). It looked like the well-known Higgins boat, the LCVP (Landing Craft, Vehicle, Personnel), that ferried troops to beaches in WWII. But it was bigger; it was designed to carry larger items such as a tank, or in our case a truck, to the beach. Two Marines were on board, in the truck, tasked to drive it ashore if we ever got there.

Consistent with the "troops before trucks" lesson from Gallipoli, our first job upon taking control of the boat was to pull away from transport in a direction away from shore and circle with other, similar boats. We were to stay there while the LCVPs went alongside the transport, loaded others of our class performing the role of ground troops, and headed straight to the beach.

Circling (or as it was called, "carving grommets in the ocean") under those conditions of wind and sea state was not pleasant. 50% of the time we were beam-on to the swells and rolling severely; 25% of the time we were bucking the swells and drenching the truck and ourselves; but the worst part was that 25% of the time we were heading downwind and down wave with minimal steerageway but breathing more than a tolerable quantity of diesel exhaust. The exhaust from the other boats in the grommet added to our unease.

It took less than 10 minutes for my partner for the day and future roommate to become deathly seasick. He went to the starboard rail and stayed there for the whole six hours until we hit the beach. He could not help when the truck broke loose and started bouncing around the well deck. The Marines and I had some hairy moments but were able to secure it. Meanwhile my partner went fully through the 2 phases of serious seasickness: the one when you're afraid you're going to die and the one where you're afraid you're not. That was the day he decided to exercise a no-longer-available option and service select Air Force.[5]

---

5. *Jack - This experience set the foundation for a personal observation about USNA textbook reliability later. 1/C year we had a one semester course that was really two mini-courses, military law and meteorology. No rocket science in meteorology; I had already learned virtually all the stuff they were teaching in that one while in high school watching a good TV weatherman. There was a prize for standing first in meteorology and I had a shot at it. But one evening while studying I read the textbook's pronouncement that waves propagate*

Eventually, at noon, we ran the boat's square bow into the beach, dropped the ramp, and watched our Marines drive their truck up the sand. Then we turned the boat over to its regular enlisted coxswain, and ran up the sand to the bus waiting to take us to our huts to get our gear and depart on leave or directly to our second block for the summer.

On the way up the beach we passed the bleachers that had been set up for and were filled with properly uniformed USAFA cadets. They were there to watch. I pitied them for having missed the education of two ordinary days at sea and one extraordinary day simply heading toward dry land.

QR9-1

tiny.cc/ca9-1

---

at right angles to the wind driving them. ▯The hell they do." says I. Well, predictably, the next day on the quiz that question appeared. I knew the answer the question was aimed to elicit and I knew reality. I consciously refused to give the book answer. I missed the prize by a whisker—about the effect of that answer. At the time I consoled myself by figuring that another competitor from Syracuse or some such place had likewise rebelled over the question seeking the book answer that the Great Lakes were too small as bodies of water to affect the weather. He had spent his childhood trudging through banks of lake-effect snow and knew better. By happenstance, later in life I lived next to an Oceanography professor whose specialty was waves. In our discussions, I brought up this right angle wave propagation business. He said, ▯Oh, yeah. That was my thesis advisor's (at Johns Hopkins) theory. He developed it by taking a big fan and blowing it on the surface at David Taylor Model Basin. Whether he blew it across the tow tank sidewise or lengthwise the waves went off at right angles." DUH!

SECOND CLASS SUMMER, PART TWO

Aviation Summer—Part Two

WHILE PART OF THE CLASS OF 1960 WENT STRAIGHT FROM DAM NECK to the aviation portion of its summer, others went off on a 30-day leave.

Those who went on leave reported back to Bancroft with a little more than a week left in July.

They were housed there for a week while they went on daily trips to various Navy facilities including The David Taylor Model Basin (the main one, not the branch now on the North side of the Severn); some computer facility proudly boasting IBM's latest vacuum-tube powered monstrosity and its even more monstrous but necessary air conditioner; the Philadelphia Navy Yard for serious fighting of hot raging fires on the surface of on knee-high, 25-foot diameter tanks of fuel oil; and, the Navy/NASA human centrifuge near Naval Air Station, Willow Grove, Pa.

Next it was off to Jacksonville, Florida (a/k/a Jax) for a week of observing squadron life, taking a one-day ride on either a blimp (out of Glynco, Georgia) or a diesel submarine (out of Mayport; 5 dives and, thankfully, 5 surfacings) and attending more instructional lectures. At one of the lectures, in Jax or maybe Pensacola, we were let in on a then-secret program flying spy planes, U-2's, over the Soviet Union. '60 was even shown detailed photos of work underway at a Soviet shipyard. But probably the most instructive part of that tidbit didn't mature until a month before '60's graduation when a U-2 (piloted by Francis Gary Powers) was shot down. That lesson loomed behind every news article containing our government's initial denial of the program.

In one lecture the instructing officer was aided by someone who had to be high among the most attractive women in the service. After she left the room a Marine major spontaneously cautioned the unusually attentive audience that she was "above your paygrade." Notwithstanding his dismissive assessment of our status, '60 Mids as a class had other memorable times in Jacksonville including an outdoor sunset dance on the patio of the Prudential Insurance Company's regional headquarters on the banks of the St. Johns River. Of course, as always, individuals had some memorable moments not experienced by the class as a whole. We'll mention one in our chapter on Discipline, Demerits, and Discharges a bit later on.

From Jacksonville it was on to Pensacola for 3 weeks of honest-to-goodness flight training.

The class had done the Dilbert Dunker bit (think strapped in an airplane cockpit sliding down rails and turning upside down underwater as in *An Officer and a Gentleman*) back in Annapolis, outdoors while the pool temperature was below 50°. At Pensacola there were two other emergency procedures drills—one was diving (parachuted) out of an anchored but motor-running T-34, through its prop wash, practicing to avoid the tail surfaces, and into a trampoline where the plane's right wing should have been; the other was for exiting a jet in an explosion-powered ejection seat (the force of the propelling under-seat explosion was such that each Mid was actually awarded a membership card in the "OMIAS Club").

Then '60 Mids flew, front seat, 8 separate hours in a T-34 (pictured) with lots of aerobatics, touch and go landings including on grass fields, and back-at-the barracks quick-draw competitions to see who could get his barf bag out of the right shin pocket of his flight suit fastest.

The Mids never soloed in any of the aircraft, but depending on his confidence in his student, each instructor tried to make the 8th hour a virtual solo, giving his charge instructions in the briefing room and walking with him, keeping as silent as safety permitted through drawing and donning parachutes, filing a flight plan, preflighting the aircraft, getting in, obtaining the required radioed permissions from the tower, taxiing out, taking off, and proceeding through the planned flight.

They Mids also had instruction time in a couple of other birds.

They had 2 hours in a Bell 47 helicopter (think M*A*S*H) during which they did a few auto-gyration (i.e., loss-of-power) landings.

'60 Mids had a bit more passive 2-hour ride in a T-28, a trainer modeled after the WWII Grumman Hellcat. On that one most flew west along the coast at about 1000 feet and over a small bay where they saw the late afternoon array of sharks, ringed at the entrance to the bay and spaced with the regularity of birds on a wire, waiting for the outgoing tide to carry the fishing boats' discarded by-catch to them. But the enormous size of the engine driving that plane came with the drawback of producing an awful lot of heat for a Florida August afternoon. So they soon had to leave that altitude for higher, cooler air. Adiabatic expansion, remember?

And they got a back seat 2-hour joy ride in a T2V, the trainer version of the straight- winged jet, the Lockheed P-80. That was quite a kick in the summer of '58 as commercial jets (other than the small, short-lived, and failed De Havilland Comet) had not yet flown passengers. On the T2V most got a bit of stick time doing such things as a loop, a barrel roll, and trying to keep a flight glove floating motionless in the air within the cockpit at the top of a zero-G parabola. Most flew over to New Orleans and back getting a clear view of the clearly older-and-browner-than-the-rest-of-the-city Latin Quarter, the Vieux Carré, from 30,000 feet.

On the recreational side there were volleyball and softball games (one lesson: don't slide on a sand field in shorts) on pick–up competition basis. The USNA class of '60 fielded an all-star team for a baseball game against the aviation OCS students and won. It also had fairly good-sized musters at the club on Sunday afternoons. The highlight of one was grabbing 3-foot baby hammerhead sharks by the "ears" and flinging them from the shallows onto the beach. Ah, youth.

After three weeks it was back to Bancroft for Second Class year.

This is a bit out of sequence, but it is the best place to mention that '60's aviation instruction continued back in Annapolis. In the spring the class had several hours training flying the venerable N3Ns taking off from and landing on the Severn. It was a Navy-designed and Navy-built open cockpit, pontoon equipped bi-plane. A picture follows; an N3N with the Naval Academy in the background:

Photo by Howard Levy, courtesy of Smithsonian National Air & Space Museum

It had a top speed of 72 mph (you could race a truck on the Bay Bridge and lose), a stall speed of 28, and a maximum altitude of 3200 feet. It featured pontoons and no electronics; in fact, nothing in the cockpits or controls was electrical.

True, by '60's years the 1930s airframes, which originally had no instruments, had been retrofitted with three mechanical, not electronic, instruments: a gas gauge, an airspeed indicator, and a barometric altimeter. A training film we were shown, made before that modernization, spoke of judging speed by the sound of the wind in the rigging.

Hearing that sound would have been difficult because a Mid's ears were covered. In a "Gosport" system, the rubber-band-positioned funnel over the instructor's mouth sent his voice through rubber tubing to the funnels similarly positioned over the Mid's ears. Return speech involved a duplicate apparatus.

These were backseat rides, but '60 did fly the suckers, including takeoffs and landings from the river. '60s Mids even did some aerobatics in these aged craft. *Jack - My instructor, Lt. Max Alvis, USN, introduced me to a falling leaf maneuver.*[1]

During my brief turn being a leaf in the first spin I did have time to ponder

---

1. It works like this: take the plane to max altitude, pull back into a climbing stall, and let go of the stick. Then you were to wait as the plane slipped from side to side and then entered a rapid descending spin. With the Chesapeake whirling before you, your job was to pull the plane out of the spin using only your feet, then pull back on the stick to return to level flight. For those of you who want more of a sense of this than our words can give, there's an early 1940s Navy training film on the web showing how to get out of an inverted spin in an N3N, though one without pontoons. The video can be found at tiny.cc/ca10-1 (or scan QR 10-1 on page 82).

Chapter 10 - Second Class Summer, Part Two

that my instructor, a company officer back in Mother B, was not known for being lucky. He was reputed to have had the second lowest average ever to graduate, but he still wasn't the anchorman in his class. Then it was my turn. Well, I'm here to write about it. So Bravo Zulu, "Well Done," to "the Whale."

The class of 2020, Second Class Summer

As with all summer programs these days, Second Class summer is divided into three blocks. One is always (absent Mandatory Summer School, see Academics, *supra*) Summer Leave. The other two 2/C year are PROTRAMID and Professional Training.

PROTRAMID, professional training for midshipmen, is a 4-week session. For one third of the class PROTRAMID is conducted on the east coast; for the other two it takes place in and around San Diego. Each week of the four is devoted to exposure to the activities of a segment of the Department of the Navy: aviation, surface, submarine, and Marine Corps. Aviation includes joy rides in a T34 (thought to be so old they must have been the ones '60 flew) and a 60-Sierra helo. The surface segment, now referred to as the SWO (for Surface Warfare Officer) segment, included an amphibious assault demonstration, work in a damage control trainer, a brief visit to a ship nearby off the coast, and various question/answer panels with ship commanding officers. Mids also bemoaned SWO week as being the only one with a planned Physical Training session. After years of tough physical training at the Academy, it was painfully easy and largely considered a waste of time that could have been better spent at the beaches.

Submarine week found midshipmen aboard a small tugboat for hours heading out into the ocean. Finally, off of the starboard side something large, black, and sleek surfaced and the tug went alongside. About 50 Mids crossed over a gang plank, filed along the top of the sub, and climbed down through a hatch. They had arrived for their 24-hour cruise aboard an SSBN i.e., a ballistic missile sub, a "boomer" nuclear submarine. Even for those not aspiring to ever board a submarine again, it was an impressive experience. The captain provided an optional "qual sheet" for anyone wishing to earn the ship's challenge coin. To complete the sheet, the midshipman was required to visit all departments on board and speak to the crew about their department. Stops included tours of the reactor and engineering spaces, climbing inside an empty missile tube, seeing the "big red button" for launching weapons, observing a submerging evolution from the bridge and even steering the sub. Twenty-four hours later, the ship arrived back at her berth and those who did not desire to make a career in a black steel cylinder hundreds of feet beneath the surface of the ocean were pleased to see the sun again.

And Marine Week is, without a doubt, the dirty week. On the West coast, mids are bused up from San Diego to Camp Pendleton where they stayed in an empty enlisted barracks. The next day they found themselves in the back of 7-ton, canvas-covered trucks accumulating what felt like inches of dust on their uniforms and faces. Events included explosives demonstrations, experience firing various machine guns and grenade launchers, rocket demonstrations, tactics demonstrations, and static displays of various types of Marine heavy equipment.

Mids also took a day trip to Miramar Air Station to speak with Marine pilots and take turns flying simulators for the V-22 Osprey or the F-18. Another night was spent "in the field" at a mock town called Mount Town designed for learning urban warfare. The day was spent learning basic infantry tactics and ended with a sim-round (paint balls) battle over the whole town. Mids camped out in the buildings overnight and returned to the barracks the following morning.

The third block of 2/C summer, Professional Training, could be Offshore Sailing, the Yard Patrol craft cruise to New England, plebe detail, National Outdoor Leadership training, etc. As already mentioned, Rob did the offshore sailing as an Executive Officer. Rick skipped the sub week of PROTRAMID but did SUBTRAMID, basically a 30-day cruise on a submarine. Spencer again did SHAPE training and was a company Admin officer on the plebe summer detail. Josh had an internship as a "Program Manager" with the non-profit Ron Burton Training Village, a camp designed to enrich the lives of challenged youth by developing their character, leadership, social and educational development, etc., provided they commit to attending during 7 summers age 11 and up. It has wide corporate sponsorship including by the New England Patriots.

QR10-1

tiny.cc/ca10-1

DISCIPLINE, DEMERITS, AND DISCHARGES

THE CENTURIES HAVE TAUGHT THAT A MILITARY DEPENDS ON DISCIPLINE. And make no mistake; the Naval Academy is unquestionably a military institution. So how does the Naval Academy transform a bunch of mostly teenagers, often previously non-conformist teenagers, into people who will not only conform to discipline but, as officers, instill it in others? And how, if at all, has that changed?

Discipline is a serious business at USNA, conducted 24 hours a day, 11 months a year, for four years. But that doesn't mean that telling about it has to be ponderous. Sure, we've all heard tell of some wannabe martinet bark, "Mister, when I tell you to jump, the first thing I want to hear out of you is 'Request permission to come down, Sir!'" But even those of us who have actually heard such a command instantly knew it was an exaggeration meant for effect.

But real discipline is not fanciful. It can be rigid but it has to be realistic. At Navy it starts—and is at its most harsh level—immediately in plebe summer. While it is apparently the most demanding then, it evolves subtly over time. In plebe summer the school's expectations of conformity to its standards are low but its demands are high and enforcement is swift. As the 4 years wear on, expectations are higher, more often met, and corrections are less frequent. But the severity of corrections, when they are needed, is often elevated as a function correlated to those expectations. Serious offenses unwelcome among plebes but punished with tolerance can, among the higher classes, be dealt with more severely, up to expulsion, notwithstanding that by those later dates, the Navy has a larger monetary investment in the disciplined person.

So let's start with '60's plebe summer. Plebes that year, as in all years, came to Annapolis with widely varying degrees of readiness for the military's ways. Some came from the fleet or the Marine Corps and were fully prepared. Some came from military prep schools; they were less, but somewhat, ready. Some came directly from a high school and had never even thought of shining—really shining, extremely high-gloss spit shining—their shoes, or considered being on time—really on time.

Punishments for deviating from requirements—even requirements with a considerable subjective component, like the degree of shine a shoe requires—were prescribed in the Academy regulations which also set forth the punishment. For example, the punishment for the first offense for a uniform's non-conforming appearance, such as insufficiently shined shoes, was "5 and 1" meaning 5 demerits and 1 hour marching. The marching was conducted at 5 a.m. on every weekday until a Mid's total was reduced to zero. If, by week's end, hours remained, up to 3 hours were marched off on Saturday afternoon. If the plebe's slate was still not clean, his remaining hours would roll over to Monday, and so forth.

Likewise, if a plebe was not somewhere when a bell declared he should be, he was awarded 5 and 1 provided he arrived tardy but within the first 3 minutes. After that he got 15 and 3 for being absent.

There were some anomalies in the demerit/hours structure. The school used neatness and shoe luster as particularly frequent causes for discipline. And while all other entries on the punishment schedule did not share this feature, violations of the uniform standards meant a scale of progressive punishments. The second offense earned 5 and 2, then 5 and 3, ... up to 5 and 5. Beyond that, offenders continued to earn 5 and 5.

One Mid having carry-over hours after his Saturday marching off his 5 and 5 "awards" barely over slept his 5 a.m. Monday date. He hurriedly but carelessly donned a uniform and chased after the platoon of classmates also in the carryover category. He was intercepted by the aforementioned Tanktracks Patton, advised that he was absent, and cited for violation of uniform regs. It wasn't 0505 on Monday and he had won a 15 and 3 and a 5 and 5. The week had barely started and he knew where he would be at sunrise every morning at least until a week Tuesday. After telling him he "should have stood in bed" the future General gave him a life's lesson by commenting, "Son, there's some days you just can't make a nickel."

At the end of plebe summer the demerit and hour slate was wiped clean. Starting with the Academic year plebes were allowed 300 demerits until the next spring's graduation day. In subsequent years the allowed total was progressively less: 250 in 3/C year, 200 in 2/C year, and 150 as a 1/C. This progression was less daunting than it seemed. After all, each year a Mid had fewer people (upperclassmen) to judge him. Still, exceeding the permitted total equaled expulsion.

The details of how the system worked deserve note. A person with authority (an upperclassman, an officer, or a faculty member) who observed conduct or a condition deserving discipline would fill out a report, a Form-2. It found its way to Battalion headquarters where the offending Mid was entitled to enter his defense on the form. Extenuating circumstances were possible; a previous dental visit running over its intended time might excuse a late-for-class Form-2. But successful defenses were usually more theoretical than real. Then the Battalion Officer would consult the Reg. Book's schedule, assign demerit and hour consequences, and pass it onto his staff for scheduling the marching obligation.

The offenses listed so far, the kinds that merited 5 and 1, 10 and 2, and 15 and 3 were Class B offenses. More serious offenses were Class A offenses. They generally earned the perp 75 and 30, not 30 hours marching, 30 days mustering at his Battalion Office every half hour when not otherwise scheduled. Mids who earned one of these was said to have won a Black N. Possession of alcoholic beverages, far more common than detected, could earn a Black N. So too could leaving your room without locking your confidential documents safe.

In researching this we found that one member of '60 had survived plebe year with an almost unheard of record of no demerits, but picked up his first for being 14 minutes late back to Bancroft after a dance. He was awarded 35 and 7 for that. Thirty-five demerits was an unusual quantum. What was that, a Class A-?

The phraseology used in the Form-2s was interesting. Many offenses were standard with pre-baked descriptions. Often they involved a generic category followed by a particularization. A generic charge for a deviation from standards for uniform might be followed by a specific of "shoes, not shined" for example. The military's librarian-like fondness for noun-first descriptions, first noted above in connection with Meals, Ready to Eat, infected these charging documents.

On one occasion in '60's time a Mid in the 5th wing was messing with a little toy truck and set it on fire. When he became concerned about the smell, he decided to set it out on his limestone window ledge to burn itself out. No problem, right? But a Mid passing by outside thought an alarm was appropriate and ran back to his home 6th wing, where he knew the location of an alarm box, and pulled the lever. The resulting hubbub, fire trucks racing across campus to the 6th wing, finding they were in the wrong place, packing up and zooking over to the 5th elevated a nothing into a something. The Form-2 read, "Fire, setting of, to truck, toy, rubber."

Another similar write up doesn't require as much preliminary description. It read, "Breast, fondling of, at hop, formal."

Sometimes a standard description could fit an unintended circumstance. It often happened that a between-class studying Mid ran late and, to be on time for march-to-class formation but also to meet room neatness requirements applicable when Mids were absent, swept up all the stuff scattered on his desk and crammed it into his laundry bag on the way out the door. The standard write-up for that was "Articles, adrift in a laundry bag." A legend, we believe apocryphal, held that a Mid was charged with "articles adrift" ...when apprehended *in flagrante delicto* by a tolerant but politically incorrect officer when in a darkened room romance with an employee of the base laundry.

Such were the mental inventions common in an all-male dormitory.

The largest one-day accumulation of demerits in the Class of 1960 befell a worthy during second class summer in Jacksonville. The Mids were housed in standard war-time, two-story, wood-framed barracks, denominated above its paygrade as a Junior Bachelor Officers' Quarters. Our star, as we got the story, had been availing himself of the local auto dealers' relaxed test drive policies to have the use of a car from a different dealer every evening. When various dealers compared notes they and the Administration took a dim view. A Class A charge was in the works but he had not yet been confronted or charged when an evening caper added to his problems.

The Junior BOQ was one of several such barracks arrayed on a large park-like tract of land that served as a grass recreation which included a pool. At the end of a night's liberty our star was cooling in the pool when a thought came to him. One of the barracks on the far side of the recreation area was the barracks for the enlisted women (a/k/a "the WAVE cave"). Perhaps mindful of the dismissive comment by the officer at one of that day's lectures (See above, Aviation Summer Part II) or perhaps inspired by beverages consumed, he decided to enter that building and seek to start a conversation with one of its inhabitants.

The story, no doubt embellished before it reached us, was that, given the heat of the Jacksonville summer, the residents of the cave were not over-dressed for bedtime. Reportedly, he managed to engage a resident in a conversation when her roommate, clad in a towel, returned from a shower. She saw him, dropped the towel (probably an embellishment), and ran out into the corridor yelling, "A man in the barracks! A man in the barracks!" He bolted and ran for the exit. After a brief run down the corridor his exit required a left turn toward the door. That path was blocked by a female Bo'sun's mate version of the movie *Porky's* Miss Ballbuster. So he continued straight to the end of the corridor and dove out the window into the building's' foundation plantings.

Two problems remained: the intruder was known to have been wearing a USNA-issue bathing suit; and the bushes were the home of a family of skunks who took his intrusion unkindly.

He spent the rest of the night in the pool trying to rid himself of the smell. Yet

Chapter 11 - Discipline, Demerits, and Discharges

the following morning, when he was called in to the office to answer for the dealership matter, the officer in charge immediately had proof positive of the otherwise not-yet-identified perp of the WAVE cave caper. Two 75 and 30's before lunch. Two months into second class year, ten months remaining, and 150 of the annual allowable 200 demerit total already on the board.

The class is the better for his continued membership in it.

Of course, the core of the discipline system is the Honor Code. USNA strives, as its Mission says, to produce graduates who are developed morally, mentally, and physically. It is no accident that morally comes first. If nothing else, USNA wants its diploma to carry a heavy inference, "This person can be trusted."

The Code says, simply, that Midshipmen will not lie, cheat, or steal. Unlike the West Point Honor Code it did not and does not impose a requirement to report observed offenses. And, unofficially, it allows a Midshipman, challenged by a question, to respectfully decline to answer—the "Bancroft Fifth."

Charges of offenses against the Code were, in '60's day, heard by an honor committee of the accused's classmates to determine the truth of the accusation. Upon a finding of truth, the matter was referred to the Administration for determination of appropriate punishment.

Our contributor Josh advises that these days the matter is referred to a Brigade Honor Board (of which he was a member). Its membership varies somewhat depending on the class of the accused. It is comprised of members of the accused's class and any classes senior to the accused (i.e., no one is judged by his subordinates). The standard for judgment is "the preponderance of the believable evidence." (Note, this is the lowest of the three standards employed in the nation's courts, the others being "clear and convincing evidence" used in some civil fraud cases and frequently in lawyers' disbarment proceedings, and the familiar "beyond a reasonable doubt" used in criminal proceedings.) The choice of the preponderance standard, as you no doubt expect, embodies a decision to be less forgiving to the marginal case than the courts' criminal standard would be.

In '60's 2/C year, a 3/C Mid was correcting a totally FUBAR plebe for some infraction and ordered him to shove out (sit without benefit of a chair). In the course of this exchange he asked the plebe a question and the plebe flat-out lied. The 3/C filed a report, the process went its course and the charge was found to be true, the Administration issued a slap-on-the-wrist first-year-leniency punishment. The 3/C received a Class A for hazing.

In 1992 there was a cheating scandal involving over 100 2/C Mids and a stolen electrical engineering final exam. In the press hubbub surrounding the completion of proceedings in 1994, the headmaster of a well-known prep school near Princeton, a graduate of VMI, wrote an Op-Ed piece published in *The New York Times*.[1] Ignoring for now his unsupported assumption that cheating is ongoing at Navy, let's start with his argument which reasoned that it is grade competition in primary and secondary schools (of which he was no doubt competent to speak) that is the soil in which the seeds of a willingness to cheat are safely planted. "It would be" he wrote, "breathtaking institutional arrogance to assume that the work of 18 years can be undone in four years at the Naval Academy—at least that part of the work that has made the predisposition to cheat, if one can get away with it."

His solution for avoiding similar scandals in the future? Instruct about honor (as if USNA weren't doing that) as if that could—by his lights—accomplish what he posited as impossible for USNA (operating with what he deemed "institutional arrogance") to accomplish with its present, more intense, severe-consequence-laden approach. Then he proposed "a radical overhaul of its [Navy's] curriculum" involving virtually eliminating all grades. That would demonstrate "cheating is intolerable— not so much because it is wrong, but because it is irrelevant..." After all, no one would cheat if there were nothing to be gained.

From our perspective it's hard to imagine a more inane proposal to emerge from that scandal. Sure, there may be educational pros and cons to an ungraded curriculum and there may be a place for that debate. But not in the context of USNA's Honor Code. Academic cheating is only one aspect of a code that seeks to insure that USNA produces graduates who can be trusted. USNA doesn't seek to present to the world graduates who have been lectured and yet never been tested and whose honor is unknown. It tested them every day from the wake-up bell, through every class, and in a thousand interactions in Bancroft and the academic buildings every year.

Consider the case of an apparent anomaly in the Academy's Annual Register covering the year the class of '60 graduated.[2] It shows that 798 members of the class completed the course of instruction, but only 797 graduated. The story behind that fact is illustrative.

It seems a member of the class, late in 1/C year, was a regular participant in a cash-on-the table poker game in a remote location in the upper reaches of Bancroft. The game had a lookout, one who could by code or otherwise, give the "Sail Ho!" warning that an officer was approaching. He did and the game was instantaneously ended, its evidence deep-sixed, and its participants scattered toward their more normal

---

1. Saturday, February 19, 1994, p. 19, (accessible at tiny.cc/ca11-1 or scan QR11-1 on page 89)

2. See b.link/ca11-2 (or scan QR11-2 on page 89)

venues. The non-graduate in question was intercepted by the officer and asked what he was doing in what for him was an unusual location. He blurted out he was there studying for an upcoming exam. The officer then asked, "Well, how come you're not carrying a book?" He then admitted to the truth. The Honor Code violation process was initiated and took until after exams to run its course. There was no basis for first year leniency. He was dismissed at the start of June Week.

QR11-1

tiny.cc/ca11-1

QR11-2

b.link/ca11-2

12

KING HALL

The central fact about the mess hall, King Hall, in the lives of Mids in '60's era was that it was the time of greatest contact between plebes and upper class.

But first let's set the scene.

In '60's day King Hall had the dimensions and Quonset-like vaulted overhead it does today. It had different murals. A memorable one at the 5th Wing end was a view of the battle of Midway from the perspective of a shot-down naval aviator treading water. That evoked Ens. George Gay, the only survivor of the ill-fated attack on the Japanese fleet by USS Hornet's Torpedo Squadron 8. Another memorable feature was audible: the power of the radio broadcast from the towers across the river was such that the wires between the central microphone's amplifier and the remote speakers around the Hall picked up the signal and, though the signal was not amplified, the speakers sounded a fairly constant Morse code be-beep-be-de-beep of the towers' call sign.

The Hall fed the entire Brigade of 3600 at one sitting, a steward-attended meal 3 times a day. Most mids sat at the same table at virtually every meal every day. One exception was for Sunday breakfast, still steward served, but allowing random seating and come-when-you-want timing to accommodate the variety of different times of religious services. Another exception was seating for athletic training tables.

At all other meals the Mids filed in from some formation or other, stood at attention at their chairs until (after any announcements, and in '60's final year, prayers) the command "seats" was given. At each table there were two 1/C at the head of the table, two 2/C at the foot, and four seats on either side with 3/C and 4/C occupying most of those seats.[1]

The 300 tables were arranged two-by-two end-to-end reaching from the narrow passage by the exterior wall toward a wide central open corridor. Service was family style with each pair of tables attended by a steward whose principal job during meals was to bring food to the table from the kitchen and attend to any requests for extras. Extra milk was the most common request; it was signaled (in '60's first two years) at the direction of a first classman, by a plebe holding an empty metal milk pitcher aloft. The steward would take the pitcher to the kitchen and return with the refill. In the later years the milk came in standard cartons but the replacement drill was, essentially, the same.

Breakfast invariably started with either a pitcher of juice or an appropriate quantity of fruit already on the table. Also on the table were small individual boxes of cereal (the boxes were identical to those sold in civilian stores in wrapped packages of 10 or 12). Selections from the boxes arrayed followed in class order. Most often Mids opened those boxes by stabbing the box and cutting through three sides at its midsection, folding it open, and dumping the contents in a bowl. Occasionally, as directed by some grumpy-that-morning upperclassman, the plebes would be directed to "camp out." That meant they were to stab their box more gently, then open it without destroying the watertight integrity of the lower portion of the inner wax paper packaging, pour their milk into the box, and skip the bowl business.

At some time during that fruit and cereal course the steward would have brought out the oval metal tray of bacon and eggs or whatever the second course was that day (perhaps pancakes and sausages, creamed chipped beef on toast, or—forgive us, Philly natives—some god-awful stuff called scrapple). Once deposited, the tray made the rounds, family style, in class rank order—everyone always respectful of the needs of those who came later.

Plebes (except on the rare occasions when they were unless granted "carry on") were required to use not more than 4" of the chair, keep their eyes in the boat, and not speak unless spoken to. They were required to conform to established rules of etiquette and were occasionally asked a "professional question" about one of the finer points of those rules. As with all "professional questions," any unknown answers required an "I'll find out, Sir" response. The correct, researched answer was due at the next meal. The Mahan Hall Library (and many known troves within Bancroft) had a readily available copy of Emily Post's treatise on "couth." Yes, she did permit eating bacon and asparagus with one's fingers. Upperclassmen did not just impose etiquette; they followed the rules themselves, as they would soon be expected to do in the wardrooms of the fleet.

---

1. Obviously, attrition was not so high that an exact 2-2-4-4 ratio was likely, so some 1/C and 2/C sat next to their classmates on the sides of the tables.

Upperclassmen commonly asked professional questions at meals. Some of the answers were to be found in *Reef Points*, others were often related to something the inquiring upperclassman was studying at the time in one of his courses, Gallipoli's combat loading lessons perhaps. Those answers could be found in one of his classmates' textbook. But not all "professional questions" were "professional." Legend had it that an upperclassman got in serious trouble when he asked a plebe the manner of Catherine the Great's death (about which there was a particularly salacious legend[2]). The plebe's inquiry of the librarian was reported to the powers that be. Hopefully nowadays a plebe, thus asked, would consult the web, thus sparing the question-propounding upperclassman the Class A consequences of his question.

In 2020's time random seating at 2 of the 3 meals each day has made the next-meal reply schedule passé.

But in '60's time upperclassmen in King Hall had other ways to gain amusement from plebes. One way was for an upperclassman to vector (i.e., send) a plebe to give a "Wildman" to one of the upperclassman's classmates. In this maneuver the plebe was to execute a surprise attack on the target, immobilize him using a knee to forcefully drive his chair into the table, and then use both hands to violently mess up the target's hair (though with limited effect in those day of almost universal crew cuts).

Another way was to conduct a pie race. These events, obviously, were only possible, but almost inevitable, when pies were served for dessert. The plebes were to draw their share of the pie (1/6th) and arrange it suitably on their dessert plates. Then they were to push their chairs back a bit, tuck their napkins under their shirt collars, place their hands behind their backs, and await the call to start. At the call they were to start eating the pie by diving into it. The first plebe to completely ingest the pie, stand on his chair, and successfully whistle was granted "carry on" for what little was left of the meal.

On those occasions when a part of the band played music during lunch, often one of the selections was either the *Can-Can* or some Conga-line melody. In such a case almost all tables' upperclass sent their plebes out into the Hall's central corridor to exuberantly perform a mass dance appropriate to the music. A thousand high-kicking young men with diverse senses of rhythm posed no threat to the Rockettes.

Other compulsory performances took two forms; an assignment of a couple of plebes to entertain the company at Sunday evening meal (e.g., a Hawaiian Mid singing the Hawaiian War chant in the native language backed by a vocal band of classmates); or, a spontaneous call for a plebe to do something entertaining (e.g., '60's most eccentric and tone-deaf classmate was always ready with a rendition of the song, *The Great Ship* about how, on the Titanic, "husbands and wives, itty-bitty children lost their lives"). More common were recitations of poems such as *Abdul*

---

2. Read more at tiny.cc/ca12-1 (or scan QR12-1 on page 97).

Abulbul Amir, or *Casey at the Bat*, or *Dangerous Dan McGrew*. Variants arose in the holiday season as groups of plebes were called upon to sing *Pogo's Christmas Carol*, "Deck us all with Boston Charlie, Walla Walla Wash and Kalamazoo, Nor is freezing on the trolley," etc. [3]

We suppose, that when viewed in isolation by a humorless, judgmental authoritarian, these goings on might prompt a call for their banishment. But to those involved, including the plebes, they were part of a welcome, comradery-building relief. And they needed relief. It was in King Hall that "the buzz" made the rounds. It was there that '60, as plebes, learned that a 2/C got his foot tangled in a line during the mooring of a still-moving Yard Patrol Craft (YP) and it had broken off while being pulled through a chock. It was there that, during December of 3/C year, '60 learned that a classmate had committed suicide by hanging himself with his bathrobe sash. Sure, members of '60 took offense and often intervened when some 2/C ordered a class of '61 plebe to sing "Deck the hall with youngster bodies, Fa-la-la-la..." But, in hindsight, it probably wasn't malevolent; it was just a grotesquely insensitive effort consistent with Buddy Hackett's definition, "Humor is pain relieved."

And there were, rarely, food fights. Two come to mind from '60's 4 years.

The first occurred on the morning of '57's graduation. The 11th company had earned some enmity the year before by its take-no-prisoners but successful effort to win the annual competition to become the Color Company. On that June morning the fruit on the table was oranges. Midway through the meal a plebe from some other company was vectored into the 11th company area to shout, "Sir, does anyone have any extra oranges for the 11th company?" In an instant the 11th company had about a thousand orange projectiles incoming. When its members emerged from under the tables they had more than enough ammunition to return fire. And after that the other side was resupplied and so it went. By the end, more than half the windows in the 5th wing end of the mess hall were shattered.

The second, on the last day before '60's 3/C year Christmas break involved serious personal harm and will not be described here.

One of the rank-hath-its-privilege features of King Hall in '60's time was that 1/C were allowed to leave meals earlier than others. That would not be memorable but for Thursday evenings in '60's 1/C year. Remember, Mids were a group TV-starved compared to their contemporaries. At the signal that 1/C were permitted to leave on those evenings, the stampede out of King and toward Smoke Hall to get a good seat for *Yogi the Bear* had the speed of an Olympic sprint and the density of the start of a New York City Marathon.

The spirit in King Hall, while achieved by different means in '20's time, has remained much the same as in days of distant memory. At least this is true for noon

---

3. See the image linked at QR12-2 on page 97.

meal, the only remaining seat-assigned meal of the day.

Nowadays noon meal formation takes place in both Tecumseh Court and Smoke Park. At its conclusion the Drum and Bugle corps starts up with the Navy service song, *Anchors Aweigh* and the unit commanders shout orders to march their units to lunch. As each platoon of midshipmen reaches the doors to Bancroft Hall, out of sight of the tourists who come to witness this daily tradition, the ranks and columns dissolve into a stampede through every hallway in Bancroft that leads down to King Hall. Jim Webb, in his book, *A Sense of Honor*, likened the mass of midshipmen dressed in the black working uniforms pouring into King Hall to ants pouring from an ant hill to find a meal.

The rush to the hall is largely brought on by the desire to avoid the long lines that form behind the salad bars, and to get first dibs on the fruit that will invariably run out of fresh-looking options quickly. There is a table near the center of the hall laid out with a modest feast of desserts and breads. Along the walls are large containers filled with various cereal options, large industrial refrigerators for milk and juice, and a few Nestle coffee machines for those patient souls that are willing to wait in line. There are also vegetarian options and soups available at the small side cafeteria, Kings Court. The tables themselves are laid out with food items specific to the lunch that is to be served: i.e., chips and sliced meat to go with sandwiches, or taco boats and packets of sauce for tacos.

As in '60's time rank *still* hath its privilege, and King Hall is no exception. The aisles along the walls that contain the milk, coffee, etc. is known as Firstie Alley. By the book, only 1/C are authorized to transit this aisle; however, during food service the book is only enforced against the Plebes. For example, plebes must fight their way between tables that are filling up to get to the wall with the milk but must then fight their way back to the center of the hall to move laterally, and then back between the tables to get cereal. This applies even if the milk is only a few feet from the cereal.

Once midshipmen have obtained their extra food items, they find their assigned table and stand behind their chairs. No one sits. The Brigade XO rings a bell located on an oval stage in the center of the three spokes of King Hall. This stage is fondly known as the Anchor, though there is no actual anchor. The bell, amplified over a microphone, brings the 4000+ midshipmen to a near instant quiet and the XO calls the brigade to attention. At this point there are sometimes comments from the Commandant of Midshipmen, sometimes a quick announcement for a club or sports event or charitable program. The final announcement is noon meal prayer offered up by one of the Academy chaplains. Midshipmen are not required to participate, but all remain respectfully silent while the chaplain offers thanks in H/H own style; one Rabbi-chaplain preferred to say his prayers in rhyme and earned the name "The Rappin' Chaplin." Following the prayer, the XO calls "seats" and over 4000 chairs are simultaneously pulled out from under the tables and the roar of conversation resumes. Thus lunch begins.

The strict rules for Plebes described in '60's time now only apply during Plebe Summer. During the academic year, the plebes may eat normally, though they are still seated along the long edges while the upper classes occupy the shorter ends of the table. The conversation at the table is run by the squad leader. Sometimes he will ask the plebes for a report on current events for discussion by all. Some squad leaders have themed days of the week where plebes will read a fun fact at the top of their voice, perform a short skit, or simply tell a joke, all based on the day of the week.

Another tradition with no particular need for occasion is a "Beat Army." The plebe performing this task will warm an unopened jar of peanut butter between H/H thighs for most of the duration of lunch. He or she will remove the hard plastic lid but leave the foil seal in place. Then, standing on H/H chair, that plebe will shout "Beat Army" as loud as possible and smash the side of the plastic jar on H/H forehead. The desired result is to pop the foil seal and launch a mortar shot of peanut butter as far as possible. The very best can launch a stream over an entire table to land on some unsuspecting midshipman to a round of cheers and applause. Many don't fully commit, and the resulting sad pop and dribble of peanut butter earns the plebe shouts and boos of disapproval.

Occasionally plebes will be required by their upper class to go on a plebe date. The plebe must ask the assigned date to come to lunch with the squad on a day arranged. Plebes will go to great efforts to set up the table with a table cloth (bed sheet), candles, flowers, and a menu. They will wear their best uniform and sometimes ask a friend with musical abilities to serenade them during lunch. Subjects of dates are often significant-others of upper class (to include civilians with special permission), brigade staff members, or just friends from another company.

The holidays usher in their own round of traditions and tomfoolery in King Hall. Halloween dinner is a stark change from the normal black-uniformed monotony, when most of the brigade dresses up. Plebes, without access or money for fancy costumes, fabricate their own out of uniforms, bedsheets, and painted cardboard boxes. The best costumes enter into the brigade costume contest held in the center of the hall. Sports teams will sometimes coordinate a themed group costume such as the Mario Kart entourage or a giant caterpillar. Every Halloween dinner is interrupted with the plebes from the men's swim team storming the hall in head-to-toe body paint and a speedo. Also, the annual appearance of the Black-N-Society in their yellow blouses with a large black N on the pocket, sporting for one night their Class A distinction of having earned 100 demerits for a singular conduct offense.

Thanksgiving dinner, while slightly tamer than Halloween, finds the brigade in high spirits the Thursday before their first leave period of the semester. The jazz band, Trident Brass, performs throughout while the plebes stand on chairs and chug half gallon bottles of eggnog. One such chugging competition went too far. Eggnog was not enough so the most daring plebes started chugging hot sauce. Then one chugged a bottle of olive oil! Not long after, an officer came up to the anchor to order whichever plebe just did that to report to the medical unit immediately.

Nothing gets the upper class looking over their shoulder in King Hall more than the weeks preceding the Navy-Air Force and Army-Navy football games. Those weeks are discussed in more detail in the chapter on pranks; however, during those weeks King Hall becomes a stressful place for those upper class that have been particularly hard on the plebes. The upper class may find themselves soaked from a pitcher of water dumped over their head, or picking cake off the sides of their head from a successful "Princess Leah."[4]

While the food in King Hall is never much talked about with much positivity, the experience is a fundamental part of the curriculum. Clearly noon meal activities in King Hall are focused on the plebes, but the leadership requirements of the upper class are no less demanding.

QR12-1

tiny.cc/ca12-1

QR12-2

tiny.cc/ca12-2

---

4. A reference to the popular *Star Wars* movie series in which the Princess Leah character wears her hair in two buns, one on each side of her head.

13
LIBERTY AND LEAVE

IN '60'S TIME THE PERIMETER WALLS OF THE USNA CAMPUS WERE VERY much more restricting than they are now.

For the class of 1960 the first time a plebe was allowed to sleep beyond them was on Christmas leave, December 20. For 2020 the first time is the 4-day Thanksgiving weekend, though a plebe might have already taken his one/semester personal weekend.

After induction day the first time a '60 plebe was even allowed to set foot beyond the walls was after the Brigade re-formed. Thereafter plebes were allowed "liberty" on Saturday after lunch until 6. Nowadays, after their first summer, plebes are allowed liberty on Saturdays from 1200 to 2359.

Today's schedule of time each class is allowed liberty, the ability to be beyond the walls, is considerably more liberal than "back in the day." But while we gauge that the details of that are of interest to Mids of yore, we also figure that for the more casual reader such details are mind-numbing and useless. So we'll remit them to an easily by-passed footnote.[1]

---

1. '60's 3/C year they could go also into town on Sundays 1200 to 1800. Today's 3/C have Saturday leave the same as 4/C (1200 to 2359) and Sunday leave 0800 to 1800.
'60's era 3/C and above were also allowed a short period after a dance to escort their dates to their weekend residences (known as "Drag houses"). The dashes back to Bancroft to beat curfew were the stuff of legend or at least analogous to a Tom & Jerry cartoon. The little white wire keep-off-the-grass loops in front of the Administration Building lay on the rhumb line from Gate 3 to the front door to Bancroft and so presented an obstacle frequently too low in fact and also far too low among a Mid's thoughts at that time to be remembered and thus avoided. Think "face plant."

As underclass, Mids in '60's time could not ride in a car. Only 1/C could ride and, after Spring leave, they could own a car and park it on the Navy property on the other side of the river, under the radio towers near the golf course. Members of the class of '57 had cause to regret doing so. That Spring a diligent but oblivious Navy maintenance crew spray painted the towers. Most of '57's brand new cars acquired a red-lead-colored, measles-like patina. Today, 1/C and 2/C can own cars in the area all year long, and 1/C can park them in the yard.

In the current era, all Mids can ride in a car, or a bus, but not on a motorcycle or equivalent. And liberty is no longer limited to 5 miles from the Chapel dome; the current limit is 35 miles. That includes all of Baltimore, all of Washington, and the Eastern Shore down to Cambridge. A Company Officer, upon request, may allow a greater range.

And not just cars are envisioned in current Regs. Bicycles are mentioned, even encouraged. There is some bicycle storage space in the various basement wings of Bancroft, with the largest in the basement of the 8th wing.

Not only could all Mids in '60's time not go beyond 5 miles of the Chapel dome, they were not allowed to drink alcohol within 10. Even 25-year-olds about to graduate couldn't "splice the main brace" at the Club. The Women's Christian Temperance Union[2] may have lost the 1932 election and the battle to repeal the Volstead Act, but it still had power. God forbid that the precious young men at our service academies should be soiled by demon rum! Mids in those days heard rumors that the WCTU did not have equal success at institutions of higher learning not funded by Congress. Thankfully, the reach of these grand old ladies did not follow the Brigade to away football games, on leave, or on summer assignments beyond the 10 miles.

Today the Regs are more tolerant of such beverages. To simplify, it can be generally said that if it's legal under state and local law, it's legal at USNA, just not in Bancroft. Company and Battalion level "socials" serve beer and wine at locations in

---

In 2/C year '60 added Wednesday liberty after class until evening meal formation to the available free time. 2/C in '20's era are allowed liberty Friday 1530 – 2359, Saturday 0900 (remember, no Saturday classes) to 2359, and Sunday 0800 to 1800.

In '60's time 1/C were allowed liberty after class but before evening meal every day. Some 1/C's OAO moved to an Annapolis apartment close aboard Gate 3 allowing their relationship to progress, as one classmate put it, "Beyond the ear-lobe nibbling stage." Today 1/C are allowed Friday liberty from after the last obligation, even as early as 1235, until 2359.

2. As for how the WCTU derived from the Christian gospels a need for Prohibition when those writings report that the religion's founder's first public act as an adult was to provide more and better wine to those who had already drunk the larder dry—to the end that He could keep the party going (*See*, John, c..2, v. 1-10), we'll have to let others explain.

the yard to Mids with an "alcohol chit" signed by the battalion office (limit 3 drinks). Current 2/C of age can drink at the Club and 1/C may join it. 2020 established a beer and wine service club for 2/C and 1/C in Dahlgren, the "2 for 7 Club" (a reference to the fact that by signing in after 2/C summer Mids commit to serving 5 years of active duty after graduation (or pay the Navy back for their education if they leave) in return for the following 2 more years of "free" education. Mids of age in any class can now gather for a few cold ones anywhere beyond the campus including at the many taverns within a 9-iron shot of Gate One.

In '60's time some Mids were allowed weekends away: three for 1/C, one for 2/C. Now the Regs permit twelve per semester for 1/C, eight for 2/C, five for 3/C and one (again per semester) for 4/C. They have to be back for military obligations (including home football games). There are wrinkles to these rules, extra weekends can be merited and routinely available weekends may be disallowed for substandard academic, military, or physical performance. All that is spelled out in the Regs.

The Regs also allow current Mids of all classes not on liberty to be as much as a few miles outside the walls if they are "running or jogging"[3] but not walking or bicycle riding. They can go on 5 specified routes described and illustrated in the Regs. That can be at any otherwise free time between sunrise and sunset, in issue athletic gear, but with no entry into any building on the route other than for rest room use. To give you an example of how far from the walls a plebe can wander—when he or she chooses and schedule permits—we submit the following, a picture from the Regs of one of the 5 routes:

---

3. To '60, that concept is totally foreign, but remember their time in the Yard was over fully 17 years before Jim Fixx published *The Complete Book of Running* and turned an activity for a few into a national health obsession. Incidentally, Mr. Fixx died 7 years after the book was published, of a heart attack, while running.

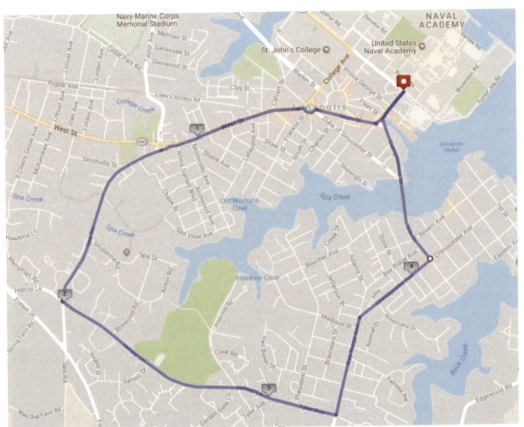

The deadlines for expiration of liberty in '60's days were absolute, carrying the threat of discipline for absence in the case of a 3-minute overrun. Nowadays a Company Officer can grant a 12-hour extension (not to encroach on class time) to allow reasonable flexibility for unforeseen situations such as a flight cancellation or a disabled car on I-95. Available permission, it seems, is now recognized as making more sense than forcing speeding or other unwise responses to stress from discipline-only deadlines.

14 HAZING

As if to prepare to coddle the Class of 1960 when the Brigade returned, on August 10, 1956 Congress passed an anti-hazing statute specifically aimed at the Naval Academy. Entered in the U.S. Code as 10 U.S.C. §8464, it provided "(a) In this Chapter, the term "hazing" means any unauthorized assumption of authority by a midshipman whereby another midshipman suffers or is exposed to any cruelty, indignity, humiliation, hardship, or oppression, or the dispensation of acknowledgement of any right."

As far as we are aware, no member of 1960, or any upperclassman, ever heard of that law. However, nowadays hazing is defined in Mid Regs, Section 3.2; it not only prohibits hazing, but makes it an offense to "consent to acts of hazing being committed upon them," or fail to report any such acts known to them.

So what practices actually used in 1956-60 might a concerned citizen consider a violation of the statute?

Eating all meals with no more than 4" of one's rear on the chair was universal and thus, probably not "unauthorized" within the meaning of the statute. So too was hitting a "brace," rigid attention, and pulling one's chin in so as to make as many "chins" as possible.

But the "Do you bet your ass?" custom was not hazing in '60's day as it was consensual, not mandatory. (Today, consent is not a defense for the upperclassman, giving it is an offense for the plebe, as noted above.) The "ass betting" went like this: An upperclassman might ask a plebe a legitimate "professional question" but receive an answer he knew to be wrong, or at least believed to be wrong. He might ask the "Do you bet..." question. It was a challenge. If it were accepted, and if the plebe was in fact wrong, it was time for the upperclassman to collect the bet. The plebe was obliged to go out in the passageway (where there was enough room) bend over, grab an ankle with one hand and protect his private parts with the other. The upperclassman was at liberty to take a large hard-cover, issued, *Navy Song Book* or the larger harder-covered, issued, *Hammond Atlas*, and, with a running approach, mightily swat the loser's fully clothed rear end. At that point, the chastised plebe was to leap in the air shouting "Beat Army, Sir!"

It would have been impertinent for the plebe, certain of his answer, to say "I will if you will, sir," though surely many thought of it.

There were physical demands made of plebes as discipline for some answer, conduct, or appearance that an upperclassman thought substandard. Generally, push-ups were not one of them. The most common demand was "shoving out," i.e., assuming a seated position without the benefit of a chair. The plebe was to hold that position until his thighs could no longer maintain it. Next most common was "hitting the green bench"—much like shoving out but with the aid of a back for the imaginary chair, the green wall of the room.

Less common was "sweating a penny to a bulkhead." In that task, a plebe pushed a penny onto a wall with his nose. Then he strained until his body heat, transmitted through the little copper, heated and thus lowered the pressure of the air

between the coin and the wall. He then was to maintain the strain as sweat ran down his nose onto and around the coin. When he felt the sweat had deposited enough salt to seal the low pressure area behind the coin such that the coin would remain, he was free to back off (at the risk that, if he were wrong, he'd have to retry).

Rarer still was "hitting an asymptote." In that challenge a plebe was to get on a bed ("rack"), arch himself above the bedding between his hands on the pipe-equivalent of a headboard and his feet on the foot pipe. Again this position was to be maintained until that was no longer possible. Obviously, this presented a different challenge for one of minimum height (5'4') than it did for one of maximum height (6'6"). But in neither case was it easy.

Another was a "uniform race." In it a plebe was directed to compete either against a classmate, or against a three-minute egg timer. He was to return to his room, make a complete change of clothes, and return dressed to inspection standards, to the timing upperclassman's room. Most often the required change was from either dress blues or a go-to-class uniform into dress whites. That required not only a change of garment, but a change of shoes *and* garters-suspended socks.[1] Woe betide any unprepared plebe who did not have a highly starched dress white uniform already rigged with the 8 individually-inserted brass buttons waiting in his locker. The worst form of this race involved two heats, classroom dress to whites, whites to dress blues which added a second sock change and the two-brass-fixture attachment of the detachable shirt collars of the time.

Such "races" continue today in Plebe summer (during idle, a/k/a grey, time) with regard to uniforms, bunk-making, and similar challenges.

Other upperclass-demanded tasks testing the boundaries of hazing involved multiple plebes.

Sometimes multiple-Mid hazing events were spontaneous, inspired by outside events. One resulted from the war started by the Israeli, English, and French forces against Egypt in October of 1956.[2] An upperclassman assembled a group of plebes, told them to assume they were now part of a Palestinian Army, and sent them to their rooms to come back dressed in whatever they thought a uniform, "Whiteworks A-rab," would look like. Soon a platoon of sheet-wearing, towel-headed, M-1-shouldered plebes was marching down a corridor in Bancroft singing songs their upperclass commander deemed appropriate.

More pre-packaged forms of collective activity were also available.

One was called "carrier ops." It involved a mattress in the corridor, an upperclass

---

1. We don't know what it is with Administrations over the years and garters. By the time 1960 was graduating, over-the-calf socks with sufficient elasticity had become common. So it was that '60 abandoned garters the day they were commissioned. Yet at USNA garters have persisted. In the 1990s Mids wore garters connecting the top of their socks to the bottom of their shirts, ostensibly to keep one up and the other down. By the time the males in the class of 2020 arrived somebody figured out that socks didn't need garters to keep them up so USNA introduced shirt hold-down garters that stretched all the way down from the shirt attachment to a loop around each foot. You could tell who was a male USNA Mid on a crowded beach wearing even a non-issue bathing suit because he had a tell-tale absence of leg hair on a precise strip on the outside of both calves.

And '60's mids didn't have, or need, any shirt hold-down device. Each Mid received a tight tuck from a roommate before either ventured out of the room. By "tuck" we mean the roommate would pinch the side seams of the dressing Mid's shirt and forcefully pull them out and to the rear while the dressing Mid zipped and buckled—all to the end that the appearance was of flat abdomens and narrow waists.

2. The Israelis wanted space. The English and French wanted the Suez Canal back. The U.S. and the USSR jumped in and told the attackers that, in the post-WWII world, they could only go to war if the big boys said they could. They told the attackers to go home. They did.

Landing Signal Officer—often equipped with a pair of ping-pong paddles, tennis rackets, or the like—and plebes in the landing pattern running toward the "carrier" and heeding the paddle command to either land (belly flop onto the mattress) or go around. Nowadays "carrier ops" are generally reserved for the run up to the Air Force or Army games. But they have advanced with the addition of a ship collision aspect. The passageway is mildly flooded with a layer of soapy water, there are two mattress "carriers" so positioned as to be facing each other at a distance, and the aircraft (the Mids) try to use their bulk and speed at landing to impart sufficient momentum to the "carriers" as to cause a collision.

Another was called a greyhound race. For it plebes were required to report wearing whiteworks trousers or sweat pants, gym shoes, tee shirts and carrying a jock strap. One member of the group, usually slight and fast, was chosen to be the rabbit and was given a modest head start. His job was to escape. The rest were the greyhounds, ordered to wear the jock straps on their faces as dogs in a race would wear a muzzle. Their task was to pursue the rabbit, barking and howling as they went, catch him, and return him, unharmed, to the starting point.

These sanity-preserving bits of insanity were not entirely one way. On "hundredth night" (one hundred nights before graduation) in the spirit of turn-about-is-fair-play, the 1/C submitted to the ministrations of the plebes in an evening of role-reversal. The hundredth night tradition endures. Also in the late spring, plebes within a company would occasionally assemble well before reveille, barge into a 1/C-man's room, overpower him, carry him outside, and deposit him either in the river or the natatorium.

The attitude towards hazing at other colleges has no doubt changed over the years. From a means to "toughen" up the fresh meat, to a frowned upon practice that is both degrading and dehumanizing. The change has been a steady march in the direction of zero tolerance; however, rumors still circulate that hazing is still used as a means to indoctrinate new freshmen. Every year, it seems, some fraternity at some college has the misfortune of having a pledge, forced to drink an alcoholic beverage in excess, die.

It is a common misconception among civilians, both college students and adults, that the Academy uses discipline as a formalized means to haze incoming midshipmen. That is decidedly not the case. *(Jack – and it wasn't true in '60's day.)*

While training in Plebe Summer and follow-on training during the academic year are stressful, they are just that, training. All activities that take place under the name of training are strictly designed to build future officers morally, mentally, and physically. The Academy is now proving every day that better midshipmen and officers can be made through "pressure with a purpose."

Chapter 14 - Hazing

Rob – There are, on rare occasions, exceptions. One case I heard about through the rumor mill involved a first class midshipmen who took training his plebes very seriously. The incident in question occurred while he was leading a morning workout for the plebes in his company. The workout was intended to be a "beat down" which meant there was a lot of what I referred to earlier as "pressure with a purpose." At one point one of the plebes threw up his dinner from the night before. Instead of giving the plebe a minute to get himself together, the first class ordered him to roll in his emission.

Clearly, this order crossed the line from "pressure with a purpose" to hazing. The investigation went for months and determined that the act was hazing. The first class showed remorse and had an excellent record up to this point. He was not expelled but was denied the right to graduate on time. He spent an additional 6 months restricted to the Academy and graduated the following December.

PRANKS

PERHAPS THE HUMAN SPIRIT HAS A YEARNING FOR DISORDER THAT cannot be suppressed entirely, even by military discipline. Whatever. Midshipmen are driven to pranks.[1] Their pranks come in discreet sizes.

Small

These are often pulled off by a single person and not written in any annals. Consider for example, the one in which a new 3/C, in retribution for hazing the year before, went to a fish market, acquired the rankest finned cadaver in inventory, returned to Bancroft and placed it above the high, suspended ceiling light in his former tormentor's room. There its stench grew ever more pronounced until it was found 5 days later.

Some one-off small pranks become running pranks. For example, in '60's era the Mids had a general distaste for obsequious conduct by classmates "brown-nosing for a grade" and so made sure that the bronze-green nose on Tecumseh's statue was

---

1. Their pranks are only distant kin to those Chris Miller gathered at the Alpha Delta Phi house at Dartmouth, either in 1962 while he was a resident (used for his movie *Animal House*), or in 1989 when he returned to confirm that the tradition remained for his September article, "Return to Animal House" in *Playboy*—ironically the same issue that reported on the USNA magazine, *The Log* and its *Playboy* parody issue, *Playmid*. Mid's pranks are not in the tradition of Mack Sennett or *Animal House*. Their themes are more subtle, more school-specific, and more in the tone of the humor of Johnny Carson, Mark Russell, or Garrison Keillor.

shined on a weekly basis to remind those marching past it on their way to class to put their effort into succeeding on the merits. Another example involves the statue of Bill the Goat, a bronze, athletic-themed statue unveiled in '60's time by the Admiral's wife. It was on a high pedestal then and all assembled had a full view of its anatomically correct underside portions of its genitalia were painted blue and gold. Bill is in a lower, new position now and that portion of its anatomy often gets the Brasso treatment long ago given to Tecumseh's schnoz. (*Photo by Debbie Latta, Courtesy of the USNA Alumni Association and Foundation*)

A popular small but multi-perp, oft-repeated prank in '20's time was to wall an upperclassman in. A victim would open his or her room's door in the morning and find H/H exit blocked by a wall, a pyramid, of something—often plastic "Solo" cups filled with water and reaching beyond the height of the door. Our contributor, Rick, was known for frequently rallying the plebes to do something by his enthusiastic challenge to "grab this bread" his way of saying "complete this task" much in the manner of "seize the day," "carpe diem." One morning he found his door blocked by a stack of hundreds of purloined-from-the-mess-hall packages of King's Hawaiian Dinner Rolls. The plebes who pulled this one off sent him an email with their group picture in front of the stack and a caption, "Hey, Mr. Bryant, Seize this Bread."

Medium

A group of Mids is usually involved in pulling these off.

Consider the plebe reprisal against the same dude as in the fish-above-the-light example above. His 2/C oppression of the plebes over whom he reigned was worse than what he had experienced. They didn't wait until the following year for their reprisal. During the course of a greyhound race he had convened, and upon a call of "Turn 9" (from within the barking ranks), about 30 plebes took a detour down a side corridor to his to his room and threw all his possessions out the window, down to the concrete landing dock 40 feet below. He knew he deserved it and he also knew that because he was hazing, he couldn't put the plebes on report without serious disciplinary jeopardy to himself. (The plebes admired and respected his roommate and so warned him at the last minute to put his desk materials in his locker and turn it to the wall.)

But perhaps a less malevolent example is the one from the late 1990s that prompted protest posters "Free the 19th Company" in the Meadowlands Stadium at an Army-Navy game. It seems that in the elevated spirit before the game, plebes in the 19th Company decided to enter (in the dead of night and via the ductwork) their company officer's locked office and arrange his furniture, placed as it had been in his office, out in the passageway. In the midst of executing the prank, some genius among them remembered that the grass on either side of Stribling Walk had just been replaced with sod. Some of their number were vectored to retrieve rolls of the new turf. When in the morning, the company officer started his day by opening his properly locked and normally appearing office, his furniture was where it had been, but it was on a wall to wall carpet of fresh green grass. The company officer was not amused. Unable to identify the perps, he placed the entire company on a post-game, return-to-Bancroft restriction. Thus the posters. They did no good.[2]

Our contributor Josh was part of a band from the 8th company that executed a recurring prank on the dome of the observatory near Hospital Point. That observatory looks like it contains a telescope. But, if it does, as far as we know, no one who ever saw it in use is still alive. It has a domed top (think Mount Palomar or the many buildings at the Keck Observatory on Mauna Kea). One evening, armed with black paint, brushes, and a ladder, Josh and the 8th company crew turned the observatory's dome into a roadside evocation of an 8-ball.

---

2. In the same company, in the same spirited run-up to the Army game there was another notable prank. It seems a pair of 1/C roommates had earned the ire of some of the same plebes. So, a few of the plebes "pennied them in." That meant a stealth approach to the door to their room while they were in it and the insertion of coins between the door and the jam on the hinge side of the door. The result was that the door could not be opened. Unfortunately, the occupants did not use their phones to call a classmate; they called daddy. Daddy was a person of some clout at the Washington Post. He called the school and the Commandant investigated, again to no avail. He too imposed restriction on the 19th company for after the game. After the win, he relented. But since the company officer did not, the more-unified-than-ever company experienced a bus ride south instead of a night in the Big Apple.

Grand

These may be carried off by one individual or many individuals but attain Grand status by being well known and truly memorable.

Midshipmen honor the grand ones in Bancroft myth long after the related repressive discipline, if any, is forgotten. And alums, particularly from later classes, honor the classes that pulled off grand pranks, though the honor should go to the specific folks who invented, dared to do, and did (or, better yet, did not) suffer the disciplinary consequences for them.

Such pranks have long been part of service academy life. And for those who pulled them off, they have been points of pride. When the top of the class graduate of West Point, Class of 1903, a man of considerable lifetime accomplishments and widely known known for his particular concern for his image, Douglas MacArthur, wrote his memoirs, *Reminiscences*, he made sure to include the story of the time he led a group of classmates in dismantling an artillery piece on display on West Point's grounds and reassembling it on a nearby roof.

When the class of 1960 arrived, the most recent class reputed to have pulled off a Grand prank was USNA 1952. At its last parade, it wanted to send the message to those who came after that they would have big shoes to fill. So when each company started to pass in review, every member of the class in the back rank of that company stepped out of his shoes and marched past the reviewing party and into school history in stockinged feet. Behind them from one end of Worden Field to the other were nearly 800 black shoes in a perfectly aligned row. A furious and humorless Administration mulled a response. It found a bunch of obstacles, not least of which was the jurisdictional problem that over 100 members of the class (those who had service selected Air Force) had actually graduated two days before. Uniform discipline was not possible and no discipline resulted.

One of our focus classes, 1960, was next to earn a spot of repute in that history through the daring of two small groups from among its ranks.

One group styled themselves as the Night Crawlers.[3] They started their mischievous antics in the Spring of their 2/C year by slipping out of Bancroft in the dead of night and, like MacArthur, paying attention to military objects placed about the grounds for display. In their case the objects were retired aircraft. Where sunset had seen them with their wheels on small concrete pads set in grass, dawn found them occupying VIP spaces in parking lots.

But the Night Crawlers were just getting started. Their apex caper came on a beautiful April day of a formal dress parade that was to be reviewed by the 21 Naval Attachés from all the embassies in Washington. No doubt the world's various

---

3. It somehow seems worthy of note that they, too, were from the 19th Company.

Chapter 15 - Pranks

Admirals and Captains expected to see 3600 men lined up like white, blue, and gold toy soldiers in precise rectangular array.

As all current and former Mids know, but most spectators do not, that precise alignment is achieved by the leader of each unit, be it a company or a staff, finding a tile (a/k/a "a guidon block") flush to the ground and shielded from distant observation by the height of the grass. The tiles are numbered or lettered sending a message to that leader that says, essentially, "Turn here, Jake." Once the turn is executed, a member of the party runs (or sometimes prances) forward to find a similarly numbered tile that translates to "Stop and stand here, Louie." Meanwhile his just-turned colleagues try to look like they are marching in an oblivious-to-it-all straight line while they are actually adjusting a little this way and then that, guiding to bring the whole formation up to Louie.

Well, the Night Crawlers figured that removing four of the tiles and throwing them in the river, and changing the spacing and, perhaps the sequence of a few others would have some effect. It did. There was no word for the result in the lexicon of the time; there still is none that is socially acceptable, though in common speech one that starts with "cluster" would be apt. The leaders of 9 staffs and 24 companies, whose "leadership" had never required anything more than following a marching plan that had been performed at least a thousand times before, had to—God forbid—improvise. Soon calls like "Louie, go there; 12th Company, fall out and fall back in behind Louie" rang out. Calls like that one seemed to work best.

Sadly, the Administration's professional investigation gave it a pretty good hunch as to the identity of one or more of our perps and, when confronted, they honestly admitted their involvement. Disciplinary consequences, long since endured by the time they graduated, followed. Their story, as written by one of their number for '60's 50th Reunion Yearbook, *The Link*, is set forth, with permission of the author, in Appendix A.

The second group of '60 pranksters, self-denominated as the Rinky-dinks, hatched a different plan and, after the event, figured a couple of honor code-compliant ways to keep the blood hounds off their trail.

Their target was the "virgin cannons."

Places all around the country have legends of something remarkable that will happen if a virgin walks by. In New York City the lions framing the steps to the Main Library will roar; in East Lansing, Michigan the statue of the Spartan will drop his helmet.[4] At Navy the legend attached to the pedestaled cannons framing the entrance to Tecumseh Court, just inside the place where parents, dates, and tourists crowd to witness the formal Saturday noon meal formation.

---

4. We suspect that the widespread existence of many forms of this legend reflects a Darwinian-imprinted impulse to suggest to many youth that virginity is not as common as some of their elders would have them believe.

Not surprisingly, they had never gone off. But at precisely the perfect moment on Saturday, April 29, 1959 in front of a few hundred observers and immediately

after the Brigade staff had marched toward the crowd and did its little intricate countermarch, then halted, one of the cannons went off with a **BANG!** As planned, fake smoke burst from the barrel. Stuff unforeseen also spewed forth. It seems 50 years of pigeon families had nested in that cannon's barrel and the Brigade staff was showered with twigs, eggshells, and guano.

This prank even received favorable mention in the generally prim and proper Sweetman/Cutler, *The U.S. Naval Academy: an Illustrated History*. However, maybe because the Administration never got to the bottom of it, or maybe because a Mid in the class of '62 repeated it twice, the details of the event were incorrectly reported there (e.g., that book hypothesizes a power cord and remote operation) and it only vaguely estimates the class involved. The Rinky-dinks tale was also reported in '60's *The Link* and is reprinted here in Appendix B, again with permission of one of the authors. Appendix B also gives an added detail or two about the investigation that brought the Night Crawlers to account.

We are pleased to report that the tradition of the grand prank proved to be alive and well during 2020's time aboard. Witness the 2018 caper of what we may call the Herndon Substitute.

For such a long time that the memory of man runneth not to the contrary, the Naval Academy has had a tradition of an event at the 21-foot tall solid granite obelisk

Chapter 15 - Pranks

across the street from the Chapel known as the Herdon Monument. The official end to plebe year comes when a member of the plebe class removes a "Dixie cup" cover placed by earlier classes on top of the monument and replaces it with a uniform cap. The task is always rendered more difficult than that description suggests by: 1) the prohibition of mechanical aids such as ladders; and, 2) the addition of 30 pounds of lard applied to the tapered granite and wetted during the attempt by upperclass wielding garden hoses. Another wrinkle has long been a totally unsupported legend that the Mid who places the cap will be the first Admiral from the class. Apparently that myth was established to encourage individual action where, after a year in a military institution, the plebes should realize that leadership, coordination, and drill are the keys to performing the mission.

The Herndon climb for the class of 1960 was described above; it happened immediately after 1/C graduated. More recently, it's a bigger deal, and scheduled earlier in what '60 knew as June Week (which is no longer in June and is now known as Commissioning Week). Climb times like 2020's 2 hours and 21 minutes are on the better side of typical.

The point to be made here, though, involves a grand prank during 20's years, what we've called the prank of the Herndon Substitute, executed by an individual member

According to the story he had considerable mountaineering experience and was unimpressed both by scaling so modest a height through collective effort. So he decided to put his cap atop the cupola above the chapel dome by himself. As the story is told, after several nights of well-planned, roof-level+ methodical progress, he did. He also decided against anonymity; within his cap was the usual identifying card with his name on it.

The Administration, horrified by the risk he had taken, their burden of dealing with parents and the nominating Congressman if he had failed, and mindful of the cost of repairs to the dome (it has since been totally re-coppered), unloaded the full weight of disciplinary sanctions on him but, thankfully, kept him in the ranks.

We, the authors, truly hope that he is the first Admiral from his class and even outdoes MacArthur in service to the nation—and that nobody tries to copy his feat. It's been done; move on; be safe. Repetition of a grand prank may entertain for a moment but, let's face it, repetition bespeaks a lack of originality.

But the risk of repetition does hold the Administration's attention. Even now, over 60 years later, standard preparation for a parade includes an inspection of the parade ground to insure that the blocks are undisturbed.

Far fewer pranks are executed than are planned. One of your authors, Rob, and his roommate mapped out one that generations must have contemplated: felling the gingko trees (or, as many in 2020 were wont to call them, "dog[poop] berry trees"). They thought about the international incident ramifications. They daydreamed those could be avoided, and the prank not noticed, if they only cut down one gender— it wouldn't matter which, fertilization couldn't happen without both. Then they thought of the difficulty of making tree-felling noise silent, disposing of the lumber, and a multitude of other obstacles that classes such as '60 didn't face: coded door entry cards, video cameras, nightscope-equipped base security forces, etc.

Even the whimsical thought that if they only took down one gender of tree, even if they were detected, their legendary status might entitle them to a minor in Horticulture did not embolden them; it merely reminded them that their daydreams didn't fit in a world of reality. In the end, timidity and the desire to graduate, not just be civilians known only to the Navy in legendary memory, prevailed.

Poor navigation or a prank? Dawn a few days before the Army game revealed that someone's dinghy had run aground at the mess hall's announcements pedestal

16 RELIGION

When the class of 1960 was in school, the Administration deemed religion essential to the School's mission.

Sunday chapel was mandatory and Protestant Chapel (non-denominational with an Episcopalian lean) was considered so central to the school's mission that the Brigade Commander had to be in attendance. Therefore, from 1845 until the summer of 1958, no Brigade Commander in any "set"[1] had ever been anything other than a Protestant. Sure, Article 6 of the U.S. Constitution that all were sworn to protect and defend mandated that "no religious Test shall ever be required as a Qualification to any Office or public Trust under the United States" but surely the ways of the service and the 'way we've always done it' took precedence over that.

Over the years some tolerance had touched the school. Chapel was not mandatory from 1863 to 1876. After mandatory chapel was restored, it was altered in 1913 when students with written permission from their parents were allowed to attend services out in town. Changing denominations was permitted but, again, only with written parental consent Mids had to form up and march to and from alternate houses of worship in town.

The history of USNA's retreat and rear guard actions of pretextual arguments and window dressing maneuvers after the Supreme Court declared in 1946 that "no person...can be punished for ...church attendance or non-attendance..." is definitively reported in Gelfand's *Sea Change at Annapolis: the United States Naval Academy*

---

1. A "set" refers to the fact that the Midshipmen Brigade leadership membership is changed during the year. In '60's day there were three sets; today there are two.

1949-2000, pp. 79-108.

Navy held fast, defending compulsory attendance as necessary to mold a Midshipman's character (Superintendent Fitch, 1948) or to prepare future officers to mold the character of those under their charge (Superintendent Smedberg, 1956). The old ways continued until students (at both Army and Navy) sensitive to their rights, and supported by the American Civil Liberties Union, secured the inevitable court decision. Mandatory chapel ended in January, 1973.[2] Tellingly, during the trial in that case neither the Army nor the Navy Administrations could present a witness from their chaplain corps to defend mandatory chapel.

But Protestant religious instruction in that era was not limited to the Chapel. '60's 4/C English class was literature. In addition to *Crime and Punishment*, an important must-read was *Pilgrim's Progress*. It is a Puritan polemic in allegorical form in which an everyman figure journeys through the temptations of life to reach his eternal reward. Along the way he is, seriatim, joined by travelers of obvious adherence to different denominations. Each of them falls by the wayside as a result of flaws in his character deemed by the author to be common failings of people of that traveler's religious persuasion. Across every classroom during that study most individual Mids saw their co-religionists dismissed as unworthy.[3]

In its class' recommendations before its 1/C year started, '60 recommended "grace" before every meal; the Administration adopted the recommendation, again notwithstanding the Supreme Court's explanation of the First Amendment and pronouncements on imposed religious expression.

While mandatory chapel has ended, religion has not left the Administrations' view of what should be. Where once the few chaplains in the yard could be reached at the chapel, now every Battalion has its own chaplain; his or her office is on the "Zero" deck of the Battalion area in Bancroft. Their services are not mandatory but they are well used. As we have noted in the second Daily Life in Bancroft chapter above, they serve (as do chaplains in the fleet) a needed, non-denominational, and often non-religious role as trusted counselors.

---

2. Gelfand reports that attendance at the Protestant service fell by 50%. The Catholics, with their "you're going to hell if you don't attend Sunday mass" teaching, lost fewer, 10%—probably mostly those with no denominational commitment but who were there to get Chapel over with early and get about their day.

3. One would have thought it to be self-evident that this form of government endorsement of the exclusionary aspect of any particular religious denomination was central to drafters' inclusion of the establishment clause in the First Amendment.

INTER-CHAPTER COMMENTARY

Youth arrive at USNA with all the diverse beliefs and expressions of their families and neighborhoods. Not all those thoughts and statements are consistent with the ideals of the nation. That observation is true of many things, including the entering plebes' view of people of different races, religions, and such. It is true as well for their views of women in the military and the intrinsic righteousness of authoritarian police behavior.

Soon after they arrive, many plebes realize that some of the beliefs and statements of their earlier lives are not welcome in their new setting. Offending statements are generally eliminated, at least suppressed, by the end of plebe summer. And sometimes that's enough because, as my sainted mother–in–law, Frances Schettino, used to teach, "Sometimes the lips say what the heart doesn't feel." But for others, suppression of speech doesn't equal persuasion of error; early beliefs live on.

As a school dedicated to producing protectors and defenders of the Constitution of the United States, and leaders of a nation organized by that Constitution, USNA now considers itself obliged to do more than simply suppress hateful speech and beliefs. It intends to do the best it can to eliminate them from those it sends out to do the work it has prepared them to do.

Perhaps the school always had that obligation. But, as Gelfand's *Sea Change at Annapolis* illustrates, historically the school has heavily tilted toward protecting what is, and away from being a place quick to implement what should be—even if that "should" is found or implied in the nation's founding documents. During '60s years at Navy on matters of race the school was trying to conform to the direction set when, in 1948, President Truman made it national policy to eliminate segregation in the Armed Forces. But it was doing so slowly.

Slowly or not it was way ahead of a nation that wasn't yet detectably moving on this issue either. The class of 1960 was sworn in 7 years before Dr. King called on America to "rise up and live out the true meaning of its creed: 'We hold these truths to be self-evident, that all men are created equal.'"

And, in those years, consideration of matters of gender equality was only a momentary blip on the radar.

On both issues the national efforts, and USNA's effort, have gained momentum since then. As always, perfection is rarely achieved.

The best we can do here is tell of the school's effort and report on the apparent, encouraging, interim results.

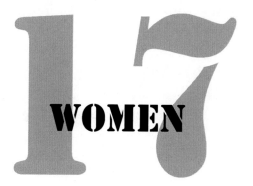

WOMEN

PLEASE INDULGE A CHANGE. FOR MOST OF THIS BOOK WE HAVE CHOSEN the style of a third person narrative with an occasional, identified, personal observation. For this topic that doesn't work; the discussion contains too much opinion. The holder of those opinions ought to own up to them. So, here they will. Jack, speaking for himself and not trying to state the views or observations of his class, will take the "how it was" section. Then Rob will take the "how it is" from a male's perspective and Spencer will take "the how it is" from a female's perspective.

Jack:

When this project started I expected to be writing proudly of USNA in our class' time. Throughout the effort that has been true. On this topic, not so much.

During our years at USNA, individually we had our sweethearts[1] and we

---

1. But of course, breakups happened. As the civilian troubadours of our times have told us, breaking up is hard to do even though there must be fifty ways. In the military it hits a bit harder. Military romances are not equilateral. The service man's dreams of his honey are heightened because they are also dreams of an outside world, a world away from his monochromatic setting (be it limestone USNA, dark granite USMA, or gray steel ship). His honey's dreams of him are comparatively dim being in competition with the kaleidoscopic daily world around her. It took country music to hit this one on the head in 1953's oft-parodied, but truth telling, Dear John. which can be viewed at tiny.cc/ca17-1 (or scan QR17-1 on page 133).

At USNA in our era there was a way to cauterize the wound when one of those letters hit. The practice was for the hit-ee to post the letter on his door along with a pad of paper and a pen.

cherished them. Judging from the women I have met as classmates' wives and widows we damn well ought to have.

But, as a class, and across the Brigade more broadly, the collective culture—viewed from 60+ years on—seems juvenile and disrespectful.

Let me give an example.

Know, for background, that on '60's I-Day class members had been issued a pair of, of what? Apparel? Footwear, I guess. Each item was essentially a solid wooden shoe sole with a broad canvas strap serving as this footwear's upper. From the inventory lists given to us on that first day we learned they were "shower shoes." Probably no one ever used them as intended. If anyone had walked down a passage wearing these shower shoes, he could have been heard for a city block or a country mile. They were called Klax, no doubt a name inspired by that sound—ana-mata-something or other—you know.

OK, back to the story. Envision Sunday evening in Bancroft, in that null between evening meal and the start of study hours which, Rob informs me, still exists. Often in that otherwise silent time one heard the sound of Klax, worn as gloves, being banged together. The wooden cacophony became rhythmical and louder as a procession formed and swelled as it passed every plebe room in the company and new members joined. After suggestive but false pauses at various rooms, the marchers stopped outside an upperclassman's room and called for an occupant to come out for the presentation. The item presented was an inscribed brick signifying that his date for that weekend was the ugliest of all the dates in the company. The recipient was unofficially obliged to place the brick above his name plate, on the cross piece above his door and below the transom, and leave it there until on a future weekend, someone else qualified for the honor.

The young woman may have been a perfectly fine human being, may have gone on to win a Nobel Prize in Physics or Literature, but she was scorned by a bunch of Mids for her appearance—or more precisely said, a Mid was scorned for associating with her.

To be sure, the plebes didn't select the recipient themselves. An always anonymous classmate of the recipient served as the one-man selection committee. Perhaps he was the current holder of the brick seeking to be relieved of its stigma. And that classmate usually, but not always, had the decency not to nominate a guy

---

Company mates passing would stop to read and analyze the often heartfelt and painfully written letter. Then they'd write their often very perceptive, and as often cruel, comments on the pad. After two weeks the hit-ee was to take the comment pad down, put it with the letter, and mail it back to his former one and only.

Many hit-ees took comfort from their company mates' support but quietly, respectfully, omitted that last step. But not all.

for dating his one and only (OAO). Usually the awardee was doing "suicide duty," dating a classmate's OAO's roommate from college, the roommate's presence having been essential to getting the OAO to come to Crabtown for the weekend. But still.

Rob - This practice is now only a Bancroft Hall legend though frowned upon and as a sign that times have changed. In '20's time someone found a labeled "brick" being used as a wardroom doorstop. Its picture went around on social media. Several women "requested" that it be disposed of.

The message of this "bricking" ritual was that appearance was almost a young woman's only merit.

That message was not restricted to Sunday evening ritual fun by a collective. It reached the souls of individuals. Perhaps the worst example of that I saw occurred in socializing forced on the otherwise monastically isolated plebes. (On campus or in-town dating was not permitted until the last dance of the year.)

Someone in the Administration thought it was a good idea to conduct compulsory dances. I'm not talking of compulsory dance classes in Memorial Hall. '60 had them too. I'm talking about mass Sunday afternoon dances in Dahlgren Hall.

They worked like this. At the start, young women, likely from Goucher or other nearby schools, were on the main floor. (Dahlgren was then our armory, where our M-1s were returned after spring's last parade, where a twin 5"/38 gun mount loomed in a corner, but also where formal dances with music from the Navy Band were held most Saturday evenings. The food court and the now-a-memory hockey rink and suspended N3N were yet to come.) On the afternoons of these dances a pair of portable white picket fences were placed facing each other and narrowing toward the stairs at the Supe's-house end of the building, much like the chute in a Chicago stockyard. The plebes entered the building on the upper level forming a herd on the landing at the top of the stairs similar to the one below. The idea was that each Mid would reach the top of the stairs, descend, be introduced to the young woman at the head of the chute, and escort her to the dance floor. Good theory.

In practice, what happened when the next young woman in at the head of the line was a sure bet to someday win an upperclassman a brick, the plebe at the top of the stairs balked and set off a stampede back toward the exit . Mortifying for the girl, embarrassing (to my mind) for USNA. It would be no less embarrassing if the within-the-Hall name of the dances were known—"pig pushes."

Rob - These dances too are known only in legend. The story told includes a detail that a time after '60's when, to avoid the stampedes, mids and co-eds were assembled on opposite sides of a curtain. The curtain would be raised and each would face the afternoon's partner.

But my most memorable experience with the issue of Women-Generic came early in my Plebe year, soon after the Brigade reformed.

A Congressman from Hudson County, New Jersey— a place so political that earlier in the decade a Saturday Evening Post article had said it was a place where failure to vote wasn't even tolerated of the dead—gave an appointment to USNA to a girl from Union City.[2] This was not only a topic for discussion in Bancroft; it made news all around the country. The story was picked up by the Baltimore and Washington papers, of course, but also by The New York Times, Time Magazine, and who knows where else. In more than a bit of the coverage it was treated as a joke.

And largely, that's how it was treated in Bancroft.

A 1/C in the room next to mine ordered me to write her a letter inviting her to become my roommate.[3]

I did write her, though (constrained by lessons my militant-for-equality mother had taught) with a different message, offering to give her a tour. After all, I reasoned, we roomed by class. I embellished the message with Hudson County references that made it sound particularly informed and personal before I showed it (as required) to the 1/C before sending it. I hoped my deviation from orders would be a successful instance of the axiom, (later popularized by Admiral Hopper of new building fame) "it is often better to ask forgiveness than permission." It was.

The Congressman lost his re-election bid. The next day the winning candidate announced that he would not renew the nomination and the Secretary of the Navy announced he had decided not to honor it.

Fifty years on, in June of 2006 while attending 2010's I-Day as part of the Another Link in the Chain program, I saw flyers around campus announcing an upcoming "30 Years of Women at the Naval Academy" symposium. The flyers gave LCDR Alfieri as the contact person. I tracked her down and asked if she had ever heard of Mary Ann Bonalski. She hadn't. I told her the story and then went to the library and persuaded the librarian to pull the press clippings on it and send them to her. There's more to that story, but it doesn't fit here.

What strikes me is that here was an idea barely 20 years ahead of its time and it

---

2. Not that Hudson County was a hot bed of women's rights. Alcoholic beverage service to women in bars was still prohibited in Jersey City (and probably Hoboken and Bayonne) in 1970.

3. A letter writing order, common in those years, often to advice-for-the-lovelorn columnists like Ann Landers, is now explicitly prohibited in Mid Regs, 3.6.4.h, part of the extensive section 3.6 of 'Thou shalt nots' in the section on Upper Class—4/C Relationships. Among the many other current shall nots, upperclass are not permitted in plebe rooms except on invitation for tutoring and such. In '60's time any upperclassman could barge in, often announced only by the dramatic rifle-shot sound of his ring hitting the frosted glass center panel of the door as he pushed it open. That sound amounted to a need-not-be-stated "attention on deck" requiring the room occupants to snap to a brace.)

inspired ridicule, not serious consideration. Such were the times.

But societies do change; and rapidly if there is an underlying change of circumstance. I'm no sociologist, but it's pretty clear to me that the most profound sociological changes in our lifetimes are the product of something that happened three weeks before '60 graduated, the Food and Drug Administration approved the pill. That event, giving women control of conception, and the new discussions that flowed from that event, altered almost everything.

I suppose by this point it's obvious that I approve of the changes. I may well have classmates who do not; opinions across our diverse group vary on almost everything. I hope and believe our bonds run deeper than our differences in almost all instances.

But I will say that I remember a homecoming weekend some 20 years ago. I was standing on the street corner by the USNA Museum as the Brigade was marching past on its way to a parade on Worden Field. The Brigade Commander leading the marchers was a proud young woman. Tears flowed down my cheeks. I don't know why. They were not some cliché "tears of joy." They were, I believe, tears of pride that our country and our school had come that far.

Rob's turn:

I do not think my words can do justice to the incredible sisters with whom I have shared my 4 years by the Severn. For this reason I will attempt to stick to the facts, logistics, and rules.

> All heads (bathrooms in the language of non-Navy readers) are split by gender as you would find in any modern space;
>
> Roommates are always of the same gender but any room can serve any gender—i.e., there are no rooms designated as always female rooms or always male rooms;
>
> If someone of the opposite gender is visiting a room, the door must be propped at 90 degrees for the duration of the visit. A proposal has been submitted to the Commandant to change this. Outcome forthcoming;
>
> "Decency" must be observed at all times the doors are propped open; all fully clothed—not just in an undershirt, and, no one in

a rack or the shower (obviously);

Dating in the hall: Authorized for upper class with upper class or plebe with plebe, but not in the same company, slang for dating another mid is "darksiding;" for those classmates that grow attached to each other while company mates and feel they have reached a stage appropriate to mention, the couple may submit a "love chit" to the company officer for approval at the battalion officer level. These chits are usually approved, and allow one of the "lovers" to move out of the company—usually out of battalion. To be sure, they both receive endless ridicule. Since Don't Ask Don't Tell was repealed, there is no separate rule for homosexual vs heterosexual relationships. The general feeling is that no one could care less. In my opinion, this is a major strength, and sign of how far our society has come;

Most of the varsity sports have both male and female components. Some of the female components are only club-sport level due to insufficient numbers.

The many stereotypes that follow women in the service largely do not hold true. "Military women are:..."

Bitchy – some of the kindest women I know I met at USNA;

Ugly – No way, by any civilian standard;

Homosexual – sure, some are, but we also have gay men, today's military as a whole has a strong LGBTQ+ presence. Sexual preference is not bonded to a single personality type; consider the personality differences among J. Edgar Hoover, Anderson Cooper, and Randy Rainbow;

Physically incapable – some of the best athletes I know are women—many are recruited for sports at USNA and many are selected into the Marine Corps. I have no doubt that they could carry me out of a firefight if required;

Biologically risk adverse –While a biological aversion-to-risk factor might play a part in the responses of any untrained person, risk taking is something we are trained in; and,

Less intelligent – this is frankly laughable. There are many outstanding scholars at USNA and many are women.

The feeling of camaraderie between men and women at the academy is not limited by our genders. As much as the men who attended USNA in the '50's were brothers, so are my classmates brothers and sisters. While the transition in the early days of integration must have been very challenging and fraught with sexism, we are no longer in a transitionary period.

Here are a couple of my favorite photos with Midshipmen friends of the opposite gender.

On the left, a Second Regimental Commander, one of my closest friends at the Academy, now a submarine officer. On the right, an underclass friend, and prior-enlisted service member, aspiring to Navy Intelligence, congratulating me on my acceptance into the aviation community.

So far I have painted a very positive outlook on the welcome of women at the Academy. So let me for a moment acknowledge an opposing view. No system is perfect and USNA is no exception. There are still cultural issues that sometimes promote sexism. This is never tolerated by leadership but the act of bringing people from all over the country is bound to bring with it a fair share of immature and "traditional" feelings on the "place of women."

For these reasons, USNA has a structured curriculum of training that takes place during all four years at USNA led by the CMEO (Command Management Equal Opportunity) team, and to obviate the worst possible reactions, the SAPR (Sexual Assault Prevention and Response) team. These trainings are most frequent during plebe year but include, over the years, bringing in speakers on sexual assault and bystander intervention, and showing survivor stories for open discussion. These programs have a full midshipmen staff with representation at the Brigade staff table. Many of the trainings involve open discussion with our classmates led by midshipmen "SAPR guides" and observed by SAPR officers of senior enlisted. While they are sometimes very uncomfortable and fraught with awkward silence, they allow us to acknowledge that: there are issues; that we do not stand for them; and, that we need to explore what we can do to help prevent atrocities from occurring.[4] Spencer has mentioned the education side of these efforts, SHAPE, in connection with her summer training and we will say more about it in the later chapter on 1/C summer.

Certainly, private discussions with my female companions have revealed to me that they still experience sexism in various modes as they endure untoward looks, comments, and jokes from male midshipmen. From my perspective, the institution is taking very serious and successful measures to address any semblance of a culture that allows these actions.

The picture is of team ground fighting—mixed martial arts. Notice the woman fighting—now a commissioned Marine Corps Officer.

---

4. Jack - Unfortunately, this heavy attention to sexual assault risk is not entirely based on a hypothetical concern or long-past events. In mid-August 2020 a court martial convicted a man, a Midshipman at the time of his crimes in and around October of 2017, of sexual assaults in Bancroft and elsewhere against female classmates (and related crimes—obstructing the investigation and such). The court sentenced him to 25 years. When I read about this I was appalled. Yet, when I mentioned it to a friend, a high school principal with two Ivy League degrees and a 30-year career in secondary education, she said, "You can bet stuff like that happens at a lot of colleges with far less effort at prevention and few, if any, consequences."

Chapter 17 - Women

Spencer's Input:[5]

Rob mentioned what we all know: the early classes of women at USNA and other service academies ran into deep cultural prejudices. But we are no longer in a transitional period. The battles they won allow me to serve without having to prove that, as a woman, I deserve my place.

Still, many Americans still consider military work to be men's work. So when a woman comes along, society can still be a bit surprised. I know that from my own limited experiences as a Midshipman. Consider the time I carried my cap ("cover") through an airport and an old man asked me if it was a memento from my boyfriend. Or the time I attended a gala at a rival military academy in New York that will go unnamed. I was talking to a male student from this other school when a mildly inebriated man came up to us. He asked the cadet what year he was in school and told me I must be a very proud girlfriend. I told him I'm a midshipman at the Naval Academy. He gasped and said, "But you're so feminine!"

At moments like these, I was not wholly frustrated. Actually, I admit I was somewhat eager to correct this man, and all other people who might be surprised to learn that I wear the uniform. But now, I scoff at my lack of humility, because women have been wearing the uniform long before I put it on. I am not a trailblazer, so that a civilian's surprise at my status, while oddly flattering, is misplaced.

To be sure, sometimes the 'military is men's work' presumption surfaces in negative ways.

For example, there was an occasion on a Saturday in September when I was a plebe. I got an email that the Marines were holding an aircraft simulation display. Since I had never heard of one, I wanted to go see. There was a twelve-year-old boy there who spoke very well for his age. He said his father was the Colonel running the display. Making conversation, I asked him if he wanted to go to USNA one day. He said that he will apply, but highly doubts he will get in. I said he shouldn't sell himself short and that he could definitely get in, but then he reassured me, "Oh no, it won't be that I am not qualified, it is just that by the time I apply, they will be letting more women in, so I likely will have to do ROTC." I was struck by his words, especially how he stared me down at the word "letting." I immediately saw that it was not him

---

5. Some of Spencer's observations above were previously published in the Capital Gazette.

telling me this, but his father. As I stood before this little boy, he saw in me the future woman who would take his spot. To end the conversation, I tried the simulator, and crashed. He made a point to tell everyone in the waiting area that I failed.

I ran into another negative judgment of women in the military during my 2/C summer PROTRAMID, the 4-week collection of service branch exposures we discussed earlier. It was during the Marine Corp exposure segment. On the second day, we were doing rotations, touring weapons staged on a dirty landscape. During a break, a female friend and classmate and I stopped to look at an M-16. A Lance Corporal approached us and said, "Hey, did you hear about that female infantry platoon commander?" In a second, another Marine came from behind us and said, "Dude, I heard she already got snagged for adultery." We looked at each other, both determined to not bite their hooks.

Our not taking the bait did not stop the two of them from proceeding to tell us their list of reasons why women should not be in combat, among which included:

1. "Look, women are a precious resource. You need them for population. You could take one dude and line up nine women, and restart a population. If you switch that, you're only making one baby;" and,

2. "Men are instinctively programmed to protect women, so in combat they're a distraction. If a dude gets shot in the leg, I'll yell at him to start his tourniquet if I am doing something else, but I'll run to a woman no matter what and that's a problem."

My friend and I stood there. We were not in a position of power. We knew that they would have already concocted a response to anything we'd attempt to say in defense. We marveled how this entire conversation was completely unprompted; they wanted us to know they didn't like our presence.

These were the worst manifestations of gender resistance I experienced in my four years, and they did not involve my fellow Midshipmen, classmates or otherwise. If there is an unspoken judgment that we are unwelcome among some male members of the Brigade, I never heard it. Whether, if it exists, it is more intense than similar views held by male students at Ivy League colleges (which first admitted women at the same time USNA did) that wouldn't surprise me. But I can say that the USNA Administration's effort to stifle and change those attitudes is both admirable and, in my experience, overwhelmingly successful.

All in all, I have assuredly had a positive experience at USNA. I am also a white woman from a middle class background, so while I was exposed to many prejudices,

I was also free from countless others.

The most common question I am ever asked about the Academy, from all parties, is "If you could go back and do it all over again, would you still go?" I always say "absolutely" without hesitation. That's not because the experience was lovely; it is not for anyone. There is something to be said about how hardship and trials shape a person, for when you are the object of something difficult, you learn how to help other people in a far more intimate way.

People told me I filled a quota.

Upperclassmen joked about my breast size.

I was called "oversensitive" when I denounced rape "jokes" being told in King Hall. ("What breaks when you give it to a two-year-old…their hips.")

To be clear, for every interaction like those, I had multiple that were positive. But discrimination weighs on me and others because we never know if the person sitting across from us secretly hates us because of our gender, race, sexuality, etc. Things are exponentially better than once they were. But we have yet a long way to go.

QR17-1

tiny.cc/ca17-1

18 RACE

THE CLASS OF 1960 CONVENED ON MONDAY, JUNE 25, 1956. ITS MEMBERS had come from all 48 states and some places beyond. Given the early morning start of the induction process, most had arrived in the area the night before. Many were accompanied by parents, some not.

One who was unaccompanied was from Hawai'i. (Hawai'i didn't have an apostrophe then and it wasn't a state). He would go on to graduate with distinction, serve the Navy well for 20 years, and retire as a Commander.

But on the night before induction, to kill time, he decided to take in a movie.

The theater closest to the campus was the State, on State Circle, directly across from the front door of the state capitol building which stands in the middle of that circle. The centerpiece of one's view of that building from the location of the theater's ticket booth was the imposing pedestaled statue of a stern, seated Roger Taney. (*Photo courtesy of the Maryland State Archives*)

He was Maryland's pride and joy for having declared, as Chief Justice of the United States and author of the Dred Scott decision 99 years earlier, that under the Constitution, Mr. Scott and his born-in-the-free-state-of-

Minnesota daughter "had no rights which the white man was bound to honor."

Our about-to-be-Midshipman, an American citizen of Polynesian ancestry with cash in hand, asked for a ticket. He was denied because of his color.

It's not that USNA or its students or its Navy endorsed that practice. In fact, when next he was allowed outside the gate he'd be in uniform and it was generally understood that if he asked for a ticket and was denied, the theater would suffer a Brigade-wide boycott faster than a green flash. Such a boycott happened years later to Crabtown's Denny's (f/k/a "Sambo's") when its employees routinely refused or inordinately delayed service to any table of Mids that had a least one African-American among them.

And the Administration was totally on board with President Truman's intent when he had ordered the end to segregation in the Armed Forces in 1948.[1] For example, 5th-ranked Navy had refused to play in the 1955 Sugar Bowl in New Orleans unless the stands were not segregated. (Navy prevailed, both in the desegregation argument and the game. It beat 6th-ranked SEC champion, Ole' Miss, 21-0.)

Still, there were reminders of racially unpleasant things all around. One was the historical marker on the river-facing side of Luce Hall marking the place where, in early 1861, the U. S. Army invaded Maryland to seize that statehouse so the legislature could not vote to secede. (The same day the governor called an off-year assembly of the legislature to convene in Frederick, Maryland to debate secession. There the Army and the Baltimore police arrested the secessionist legislators.)[2]

And in 1956 Annapolis and Maryland were still segregated societies. The Civil Rights Act or '64 was almost a decade in the future and Maryland didn't repeal its prohibition of interracial marriage until 1967 after the U. S. Supreme Court had agreed to hear the probably-selected-for-review-by-its-name case of *Loving v. Virginia*. In it the Supreme Court declared state statutes prohibiting interracial marriages unconstitutional. "What freedom is more central to humanity than freedom of whom to marry?"

USNA, down in the trenches, was not as comfortable with racial equality as its leadership would have it.[3] Tables at every meal were served by mess stewards, a position apparently racially limited to people of African ancestry or Philippine citizenship. All Bancroft's janitorial staff members were men of color.

Another example is that plebes were supposed to be able to recite immediately

---

1. 1948 was the same year he ended "auxiliary" status of women in the military known as WAVEs and WAACs

2. Sun Tzu, author of *The Art of War*, would be delighted, a battle won before it needed to be fought.

3. The first African-American to graduate from USNA, noted in the Preface, did so seventy-two years after the first of his race, born a slave, graduated from West Point.

at an upperclassman's request, the number of days until the Army-Navy game, the next leave, the Ring Dance, and Graduation. They also had to be able to recite the menu for the next meal, and the movies playing in town—but only at the three whites-only movie theaters. If a plebe finished that recitation he might be asked, "And what's playing at the Star?" (In then-segregated Annapolis the Star was the theater serving the African-American community.) The expected response was not what was playing, but "I didn't know you were dating, Sir," an implicit adoption of the then-prevalent white cultural discomfort with interracial romance. Some "woke" plebes actually checked what was playing at the Star and gave that answer.

In '60's senior year a Mid submitted a proposal for USNA to establish and host a debate tournament as many other colleges (including USAFA) did. The proposal followed standard Navy protocol calling for it to be routed up the chain of command to the Superintendent with each person in the chain required to forward it with his positive or negative endorsement. The proposal envisioned a modest initial tournament, limited to about 16 relatively local colleges. The proposal was stymied by the ranking civilian in the Department of English, History & Government with the threat of a negative forwarding endorsement (based on an unmanageability pretext) unless top-flight nearby Howard and Morgan State (then referred to as "Negro colleges") were deleted from the proposed invitation list.

Such were the times. But they were changing.

The Mid who had made the proposal was offended and said so to the faculty advisor. Through the back and forth he learned a lesson about strategic retreat. The faculty advisor worked out a plan with him involving amending the invitation list as demanded but then managing the tournament well (and the Mid who managed it—not the proponent, by the way—did a masterful job). Then, in keeping with the plan, the next year the debate team put forward a similar proposal including Howard and Morgan State. In 1961, as the faculty advisor had predicted, no pretext of unmanageability was credible and the proposal sailed through. The tournament continues in 2020.

But beyond the Brigade, the Town of Annapolis, and the State of Maryland, things were not nearly settled in the nation either. In March 1960 a ghost-written book, published under the name of a United States Senator widely supported in our class and destined to become his party's 1964 candidate, declared that racial problems in places like Mississippi and South Carolina were not the concern of the federal government but were best left to the citizens of those states to work out. That assertion seemed totally oblivious of the fact that the Civil War had made "The United States" a singular noun and the three Constitutional amendments which followed it unequivocally made local treatment of racial minorities a federal concern.[4]

---

4. The book was intended as a start toward turning Goldwater's party from the party of

More importantly, nationwide TV news was covering how those folks were working it out. Scenes of lynchings, murders, bus bombings, and police fire hose and dog attacks on children exercising an apparent First Amendment right "peaceably to assemble, and to petition the Government for a redress of grievances" (the grievances being governmental obstacles to Americans of African ancestry voting) did not sit well with Americans watching in living rooms located in states other than those of the Confederacy. One hundred years after the first state seceded, things were coming to a head.

Also by 1956, a Baltimore-born Maryland lawyer, Thurgood Marshall, had been leading a 20-year campaign against public school racial segregation that had led to the 1954 decision in *Brown v. Board of Education of Topeka, Kansas* (holding that "separate but equal" public schooling is inherently and unconstitutionally unequal). Implementation battles in places like Little Rock were yet to come.

Four decades on, in 1996, 3 years after he died, Justice Marshall became the second U.S. Supreme Court Justice to have a statue in his honor erected in Annapolis, his in front of the State Supreme Court building.

Photo Courtesy of Visit Annapolis & Anne Arundel County

Lincoln and especially away from President Eisenhower who, by the ghost-writers' lights, erred when he sent troops in to enforce a court order to desegregate Little Rock.

2020 returned to Bancroft after its Youngster Cruise for its first "Hello Night" as a non-plebe. Later that night, shortly after 2 a.m. on the morning of August 18, 2017, the 145-year-old statue of Justice Taney was craned off its pedestal and trucked to storage.

His name was removed from the pedestal. The pedestal remains.

The times have changed, but not completely. After all, people with a reason to know decided the Taney monument was best removed under cover of darkness in the after-midnight hours of a sleepy Friday night. (*Picture courtesy of the Maryland State Archives*)

So where are we in 2020?

As we are writing this in the summer of 2020, out in the streets, multi-racial crowds committed to equality are protesting police brutality against people of African ancestry and the continued display of memorials to racists past. Others, seeking political advantage among resistant voters, are pointing to the protests as a threat to law and order.

Earlier (that is, late the spring of 2020) the Alumni Association and the Academy were facing intramural problems of unredeemed racism on three fronts. The cases all involved expression of thoughts incompatible with the nation's founding ideals expressed on social media—one by a member of the Association's Board of Trustees, another by a rising 1/C, and the third by an accepted-for-admission applicant scheduled to join the class of 2024. We don't have the details of the bit posted by the Trustee but know that he was removed from the Board. And the applicant had the approval of his admission revoked.

As for the rising 1/C, we and the Brigade have seen some of his authoritarian reactionary Twitter rants. Those we have seen and others reported in the press, expose his ignorant stereotypes of African-Americans as uniquely drug-using, welfare-dependent burdens and his approval of police violence, not legal process, for remedying what he perceives to be the evils of blacks in our society. As the Annapolis *Capital Gazette* reported, his "Tweets included calling for drone strikes on civilians whom he considered to be Antifa activists."[5] For the benefit of those who made read this in future years, "Antifa" is a term of the current political right for those

---

5. Read the full article at tiny.cc/ca18-1 (or scan QR18-1 on page 142).

on the left who have been protesting fascism in contemporary American politics. He also tweeted that Breonna Taylor "received justice." She was killed by Louisville, Kentucky police who barged into her apartment—the wrong one—during the late night execution of a no-knock arrest warrant for a man who was already in custody.

At this writing in the fall of 2020 the transmission of the Academy's recommendation of his expulsion to the appropriate Assistant Secretary of the Navy has been forbidden by a federal court, at least until the end of his 1/C year's fall semester. The case is still pending.

An observation: the Trustee contended someone other than he made his posting more public than intended. But such ugliness doesn't have to be hidden, anonymous, or accidentally shared. Some people expose themselves on their own. Social media often acts as a vehicle broadly exposing the cruel things people will say to a broader audience than in past years when such expressions were heard only by like-minded people within earshot. Still, when not denounced, social media messages spread the hatred.

Rick's input

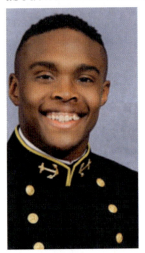

When I was asked to contribute to this section, at the time of—and so in the context of—the tweets of the rising 1/C Mid just mentioned, I started thinking about how it all made me feel. Blatant and outward ignorance upsets me, but honestly at this point I'm just so tired...I am not surprised, I'm not outraged, I'm just exhausted, because it is so much larger than the Academy.

As I started to gather my thoughts for a contribution to this effort I could not recall personally experiencing any hate-tainted incident during my time at USNA. On the other hand I was not immune to feeling the hate that's in the nation's air.

To give you some insight into how it feels and how it has touched me at the Academy, there is a social media video floating around; it's a compilation of police brutality videos, all against people of African ancestry. It's about 2 minutes long and it effectively endorses the brutality as the American Way by playing, in the background, the National Anthem. With every case of nationally covered police brutality the video pops up again, longer by the new footage. Imagine having to watch and experience that multiple times a year for a decade. But, you still decide to serve because you still believe in the country's ideals as expressed in its founding documents, not the part of its reality shown in some video.

Then in a discussion at the Academy one of your brothers in arms says to you that everyone in that video deserved the brutality he received.

How must you feel when your classmate, your brother, attempts to justify every instance of brutality in the video? Why does that hurt so badly? Those were people you had empathy for, your mirror neurons literally allowed you to feel their pain. Their pain became your pain. Their beating became your beating. So, in the conversation you see your brother's justification for them getting beaten as maybe his justification for you getting beaten.

Is it that he just doesn't have empathy for people of darker skin? Or is it that he just doesn't have empathy for people who appear to have done nothing wrong or, at worst, had committed some minor crime? And does he feel free to say to me what he did because he doesn't see me as a criminal?

Is he such an authoritarian and so ignorant of the Constitution he is sworn to protect and defend? Does he not know that the people who threw off British rule understood the horror of governmental power misapplied? Does he not know that because of that they provided a Bill of Rights which entitles all of us, criminal or not—white, black, or other—to be free from being treated as an "other" in an "us vs. them" showdown with the forces of our government?

Does he really think that Eric Garner deserved to die for being involved in a poor man's transaction involving selling individual cigarettes to people who couldn't afford a full pack? Does he think an Abner Louima, arrested in a bar brawl for disorderly conduct and resisting arrest, deserved to have a wooden stick shoved in his rear and then rammed so forcefully into his mouth as to break his teeth? Can any 'law & order' outlook justify the death of George Floyd, arrested on a store clerk's accusation of passing a counterfeit $20, who used his last breaths to call his dead mother in a final invocation before his death?[6]

Where would his empathetic neurons have been if any of these events had happened in the white neighborhood he grew up in? Can he not see the racial aspect of these events?

Is there no racial aspect to this and is it simply a matter that police have to serve as society's attack dogs and, like attack dogs, absolutely have to be well trained when not to attack? It can't be, but does he think so?

Maybe he does freely discuss it with me because he doesn't see it as a racial matter but rather as a criminal matter, and he sees me as a brother not a criminal. Maybe discussions like ours at the Academies, in the fleet, and elsewhere in the

---

6. I mean the 4th, 5th, 6th, and 14th Amendments. Does he not know that even the jury-convicted-guilty, not the merely police-believed-to-be-guilty, are entitled to receive only a punishment that's not cruel and unusual (the 8th)?

Armed Forces are part of the solution, not part of the problem. That's probably part of what President Truman intended in 1948. Are they happening elsewhere? Are there any other parts of American society—even other American colleges—where this level of social interaction exists and permits such discussions among equals?

I doubt it.

So you're hurt initially. Then you get angry. But after a while it all washes away into a gray, dull lifelessness. I feel no pain or sadness anymore. Only pity and exhaustion.

But, I'm tired of being tired. Especially at an institution built on a foundation of moral leadership. My feeling is that not only the nation, but this school where its ideals are treated most directly, needs to do a lot more and better. USNA should not be a place of reluctant compliance, as it had been on admission of people of African ancestry, on the admission of women, on respect for the privacy of religion, and on bringing its academics up to contemporary standards. Where it once followed it must now lead. And from the cases of the Trustee, the applicant, and the rising 1/C it looks like, this time, USNA understands its obligation. And, from within its ranks, I think it says something that I still truly count the classmate I had that discussion with as a brother in arms, perhaps even more because of our honest, mutually respectful, equilateral discussions.

QR18-1

tiny.cc/ca18-1

19
FIRST CLASS SUMMER

WE HAVE DEFERRED DISCUSSION OF OUR FOCUS CLASSES' 1/C summers until now lest these important, finishing touch parts of the classes' development into Naval officers blend into the recitations of the summers of earlier more fundamental years. But deferred or not, they are worthy of mention and memory.

For its 1/C cruise '60 was scattered over the globe.

For 40 members of the class (and all 3/C, class of '62) that cruise started with destroyer transport to Newport or Boston, transfer to other ships for two weeks of fleet exercises, then transit up the St. Lawrence River to Montreal for ceremonies opening the St. Lawrence Seaway presided over by President Eisenhower and the Queen. From there it was up the Seaway and into and around the Great Lakes. On the return there was a kerfuffle when a bottleneck developed at the entrance to the Welland Canal. It necessitated an unplanned flight from Niagara back to Baltimore on various Navy aircraft.

Apparently, that put the Academy's whole summer training over budget. Other cruises were cut short and many '60 Mids got an extra 10 days or so leave.

The summer experiences of those not on that cruise were diverse.

A couple of hundred transited to the Med where they dispersed to other operating units of the 6th Fleet. In the middle of the summer they were airlifted home and were replaced by an equal number who had been airlifted in.

Another group of about 60 went to the Western Pacific. They started with 2 weeks of leave, either taking naval aircraft to San Francisco to start a short leave there, or private travel to their homes for the leave period, then on to San Fran. From there, starting about June 20, they were flown on to join ships at Pearl, Guam, Hong Kong, Kaohsiung in Formosa (n/k/a Taiwan), and Sasebo and Yokosuka in Japan.

Another 70 members split into two groups went on submarine cruises in the Atlantic. A few, 5, also split, and went to the Pacific where they joined a sub cruise that was primarily for NROTC students.

The rest were assigned to cruises in various surface commands on the eastern seaboard. About half went on a fleet exercise and the rest were scattered to individual destroyers ported along the east coast from Newport to Key West.

Many of those in the Atlantic Submarine and Atlantic Destroyer assignments are recorded as having been transported by "aircraft assigned from the Naval Air Facility Annapolis." We doubt that means they flew to and from their assignments on the lumbering 2-engined seaplanes (UFs) that shared facilities with the N3Ns pictured earlier. '60 had watched them using the Severn as their runway since plebe summer. Often they aborted their take-of attempts for lack of enough airspeed to clear the then-lower Naval Academy Bridge across the Severn. There must have been transports assigned to the USNA Air Facility stored elsewhere.

Whatever the ship, each Mid was not only to participate in and generally observe that ship's routine as a quasi-junior officer but also complete requirements set forth in a handed-out curriculum calling on them to learn specific things about the ships' various departments from the bilge to the bridge.

For most, the curriculum included taking their celestial navigation from the classroom to sea. All the work with star charts and the Hydrographic Office's book of tables[1] wouldn't have been worth a hill of beans if they hadn't learned the practical trick for getting the one star they were looking for centered in the small view provided by the lens of a sextant.

In the summer of 1959 getting a cell phone position fix was not an option.

2020's 1/C Summer

Nowadays a Midshipman's 1/C summer is much more focused toward the branch of the service he or she hopes to be able to select in the next Spring.

One block is called "First Class Cruise." It is usually highly focused on a Mid's personal intended service selection and includes Powered Flight Program (PFP), Leatherneck, and similar assignments offered those considering Seals or Explosive Ordinance communities. For those going surface, the Cruise section is exactly that, much akin to the 1/C surface cruises the Class of '60 experienced.

---

1. HO-214, an Atlas-sized product of a hoard of mathematicians put to work by the depression-recovery program, the Works Progress Administration (WPA). These days it's an app.

Chapter 19 - First Class Summer

The other two blocks are Professional Training and leave (or voluntary or compulsory summer school or parachute jump school).

For those who hope to select—and be selected by—the Marine Corps, Leatherneck is a must. It is a 4-week intense, exhausting, officer training course at Quantico. It is often paired with 4 weeks integrated into a Fleet Marine Force unit. More Mids attend than the Corps has room for as officers, and in the Spring more apply than are chosen.

Rob hoped to (and later did successfully) service select Navy Air. So he applied for and was selected for a program called the Power Flight Program (PFP). In addition to aviation classroom instruction on campus he received further instruction and experience at a private flight school, Trident, at the Easton airport. It included 10.5 flight hours up to and including a solo. The photo is of Rob and his "wingman," also a USNA 2020 student, after they completed their solos.

The Trident school provided the planes and some civilian instructors, but most of the instructors were military assigned to the Academy. The PFP program had 125 slots and is believed to count as a plus when Navy Air makes its selection. But unlike the Leatherneck/Marine Corps ratio, Navy Air takes about twice as many graduates as are able to take PFP.

Most others who aspire to Navy Air apply for an aviation cruise. It involves merging into squadron life at various bases and likely getting a few joy rides and possibly a bit of highly supervised time at the controls. Josh did that program in a

Patrol Squadron flying P-8s.

This program, too, has budgetary limitations, so still others who aspire to fly are relegated to surface ships for their 1/C cruise.[2]

The Professional Training block can include Offshore Sailing, Plebe Summer Detail, the New England YP Cruise, National Outdoor Leadership sessions, and a few other things. As mentioned earlier, Rob went to sea commanding a 44-foot sloop—actually, the sloop *Brave*, the one on the cover.

Josh applied for and was accepted in one of those "other things," a one month "LREC",[3] a cultural immersion trip with a few other Mids and a USNA professor. They went to Northern France and a bit of Belgium for an examination of the battles of WWI fought in that area, the trenches, the atrocities, and the reality that history textbooks do not convey.

Rick was also accepted for an LREC. In his case it dealt with his long term interest in East Asia and specific desire to see Japan. He reports that he can't remember being so consistently happy over such a long period (his 18 days in that country) in a long time. He got to explore all over the country, talk with high-ranking members of the self-defense force, and gain a sense of the dynamic of the US/Japan relationship.

For his other block Rick volunteered for the Plebe Summer Detail which held a charm for him because, from his experience as a plebe, he viewed it as a time when routine cynicism is absent in both the Detail and the new Mids. Both can speak openly about their ideals and aspirations. Once there and to his surprise he was made the commander of the Regiment, the entire plebe summer unit. His duties spanned from the mundane (such as deciding when a drill should be cancelled for weather) to the serious (such as leading all the other upperclass on the Detail and, on occasion,

---

2. Some, who aspire to be Marine Aviators, take both Leatherneck and PFP in the hope of being spotted as unusually Gung Ho.

3. Language, Regional Expertise, and Culture. Recent ones, in addition to Rick's Asia-Pacific one and Josh's to France and Belgium, include Viet Nam, Ukraine, Inter-Andean (meteorology) to Chile and Easter Island, NATO Cyber (Europe) and Cyber (England), Israel, etc.

removing people from the Detail for not meeting standards). He also had "fireside chats" with plebes, trying to impress them with the values and ideals that USNA had ingrained in him.

Spencer did a 1/C cruise on an amphibious warfare ship, the *USS Pearl Harbor*. And in this summer she, like Rick, had her favorite training. And, like Rich's it was back at school in an instructional role and as a leader of the program. In the summer of 2015 she had attended the Summer Seminar for rising high school seniors, where those seniors are given a taste of life at the Academy. It was there that she decided she wanted to attend. Four years later, in her 1/C summer, she not only participated in the Summer Seminar, she was Summer Seminar Commander. That summer she also did her third SHAPE training which prepared her to be the SHAPE Program Commander, a 4-stripe position, in the second semester of her senior year.

20 RETENTION

WHEN THE CLASS OF 1960 WAS INDUCTED, THE NAVY DID NOT DEMAND of the mostly 17- and 18-year olds a commitment to a career. All it asked, and told those about to take the oath, was that they need only commit to keeping an open mind to the possibility. In fact, the idea that the school was aiming to provide graduates *dedicated* to a career of naval service wasn't added to the school's mission statement into well into 1960's final semester, less than 3 months before it graduated.

And that likely wasn't entirely an oversight. The school was providing a good education to 3600 students who were among only 2.9 million 4-year college students nationwide. Today's approximately 4600 members of the Brigade are students are among 19.6 million contemporaries preparing in 4-year colleges across the country.

Still, whatever the school intends in any year, ultimately the choice to stay or leave the service after the initial obligation is one that is on the individual graduate's mind as the time of the expiration of that initial obligation approaches. Most often that final commitment is made when the advice of a new person, a spouse, bears with substantial weight on the choice.

When the members of the class of 1960 signed their contracts on I-Day, the obligation set forth in the paperwork was for "not less than" 3 years of active duty service after graduation (and 3 subsequent years of ready reserve service). The Navy "interpreted" that to mean 4 years for '60. Later, in the second half of 1963, when members of the class were well into their final year of school-obligated service and some were preparing to leave for grad schools, the Navy changed its interpretation in the case of many who had been successful in school and in the fleet. It "interpreted" the paperwork to permit Admiral Rickover to draft them to stay in and attend his nuclear power school (and, under threat of additional delay of their career plans, volunteer for submarine school). Then they would be obligated to serve still more years and serve additional years to "pay" for that extra schooling. A few resisted and, relying on the 13th Amendment and common sense (why take years from only those who had served well?), they prevailed. The Navy changed the paperwork for some later classes to 6 years of active duty. It now rests at 5.

The purpose of this chapter is to contrast how the options for choosing a career looked to each of our subject classes at the time of graduation. The short of it is that continued service is much more attractive to the class of 2020.

Of course, one consideration is base pay.

In 1960 the pay of an Ensign was $222.30/month, $2,767/year. In terms of purchasing power that was 18% lower than pay for a similarly ranked officer in 1942. Perhaps Congress figured, "Sure, but in 1942 they were fighting a war." Fair enough, but the trend was not encouraging and Congress addressed the pay scale only sporadically.

The class of 2020 receives pay at graduation of $3,287/month, $39,444/year (more for those with prior service). In terms of purchasing power that's 70% better than in 1960. Otherwise put, 2020 starts as an O-1 (Ensign or 2nd Lieutenant) with no service time at a living standard 1960 would only reach as an O-3 (USN Lieutenant or USMC Captain) with 4 years of service. And 2020 is looking forward to an annual adjustment to the pay scale that doesn't require Congress to get around to thinking of it; a cost of living adjustment (COLA) is baked in.

And the pay scale looking forward is consistently higher. At the projected retirement levels he ratio of inflation-adjusted base pay for 2020 compared to 1960 shows about a 1.5 times advantage for today's graduates.

And benefits figure in, but again 2020 holds a significant edge, at least over a civilian pay equivalent, the alternative to be considered at the time of the retention decision. The slice of civilian pay now going to medical coverage beyond an employer's contribution lessens the value of the civilian pay considerably. And housing and subsistence allowances are another advantage. They are ample and non-taxable but they vary according to zip code so precise comparison is elusive.

But the biggest comparative financial advantage of 2020 over 1960 is in the area of retirement benefits.

For one thing, Navy is an up-or-out career. (For 1960 low "aptitude for the service" graduates, the prospect of not being retained for 20 years by a service that had been telling them for four years that they had no aptitude for it was not good. The prospect of even respectful dismissal after 15 or so years and therefore earning virtually no pension credits during about 15 of one's most productive years of one's life—made serving the minimum and getting out a no-brainer.)[1] In contrast, in a civilian career you may fall off the path to CEO but, assuming reasonable competence, could probably remain at some middling level and support your family.

But the major difference considered by about-to-graduate members of '60 was that the prospect in 1960 of half-base-pay at 20 years of service—or for that matter the 3/4 pension at 30—didn't have a promise of a cost of living adjustment. Fortunately for the class of 1960 COLA came in before its members retired, but it was not on the radar when they graduated. At that point even the moderately successful members of the class were looking at being kicked to the curb at about 42 years of age. Half pay then, unadjusted for inflation, would mean 1/8th pay (in purchasing power) for them at the age they are now.

Sure they could go back to school and train for a new career at the end of their 20 years. But would they have the savings to do that and still provide an education for their probably teenaged children looking toward college themselves? At least 2020 has a prospect of a more robust and marketable post-graduate education program available during their active career years and a more active alumni association assistance program finding them post-Navy placements in government and elsewhere.

The physical risks of service may have figured into some folks' consideration. The risks of combat were in everyone's calculus and had been from before the day they pledged to serve. And the other physical risks inherent in naval service were part of the commitment as well, though probably less obviously so. The Class of 1960 has 5 names on the Memorial Hall Killed-in-Action roll beneath the Don't Give up the Ship flag. But it also has 23 names on its wall plaque in that Hall listing those killed in non-combat service-connected events (washed overboard in a storm from a surfaced diesel submarine at night; onboard during a submarine's catastrophically failed sea trials; catapult launched from a carrier with inadequate steam and so shot into the sea, not the air; etc.). 15 of the 28 lost their lives before they made USN Lieutenant or USMC or USAF Captain, that is, before their 4-year, school-obligated service expired and they had an opportunity to finalize their career choice.

It must be said that the role of a spouse in the decision about whether or not to stay is a very significant one. The members of 1960 are quick to say that the toughest job in the world is "Navy wife." Even in peacetime with 6-month Mediterranean deployments, 7-month Western Pacific deployments, and shorter but more out-of-reach ballistic sub deployments, it's not easy. Still, '60's ranks include 30-year, full

---

1. Navy is still an up-or-out career. But these days there is a separation payment for those involuntarily terminated at the O-4 (Lieutenant Commander or Major) level under honorable or general circumstances. It comes with a reserve service obligation which implies the ability to reach 20 years of combined service and ultimate retirement benefits, including Tricare health and a pension of 2.5% of base pay per active duty year (plus reserve drill days credits) served, payable—not at retirement—but starting at age 60.

career retirees whose decisions to stay in were heavily influenced by wives who truly liked the life style, particularly the comradery of the sisterhood and the quality of other Navy wives they met in postings around the world.

In short, for graduates of 1960 a service career often proved to be a good life and, economically a better one than it appeared it would be as they graduated. For graduates of 2020, especially economically, it should be even better.

WRAPPING UP

WHEN THIS PROJECT WAS JUST A THOUGHT, THAT THOUGHT INCLUDED the idea that it would end with the shared experience of our classes' lifetime-highlight final weeks at USNA in time-separated springs but, commonly, in the springs of our respective lives ending in a common exuberant hurling of our caps in the air at graduation. But the COVID pandemic intervened.

Instead, we'll use this space to mention some minor things about '60's time in the Yard that are fondly remembered but didn't fit at a specific place earlier; then we'll end by describing the extraordinary spring that made 2020's final months and graduation unique and worthy of honored inclusion in the 175-year old Academy's annals.

First the little things that gave '60s years some color.

In its plebe year the school was a major stop on the itinerary of a visiting dignitary, King Saud of Saudi Arabia. He toured the place, reviewed a formation of Mids, and took in a basketball game against Duke which went to overtime as was common in the pre-Mike Krzyzewski (USMA, '69) days. On the King's way off campus in a motorcade via the rarely used Gate 2, with the Color Company lining the curbs at "present arms," the lead car carrying the press photographers crashed into the gate. Those Mids swear they held the uncomfortable "present arms" position for a world record length of time.

Early in the fall of 3/C year the USSR launched the first space satellite, Sputnik. It sent the nation and the Academy into a tizzy. A couple of years earlier the TV show *Wonderful World of Disney* had devoted 4 shows to describing the launch of a satellite, a marvelous wonder of the moderately distant future. The actual event came sooner, from an unexpected source, and was a clarion call, a "game on" start to the space race.

At the start of '60's 2/C year USNA appointed its first Catholic Brigade Commander, a truly nice and impressive guy from Philadelphia. As the term wore on, the Philly press started to hype the idea that a Philly native was going to lead the Brigade onto Memorial Field for the Army game. It was not to be. One of his classmates had smuggled a girlfriend into Mother B and when she had "a call of nature," the classmate requested the use of the only private toilet facilities in Bancroft, right down the hall from the smuggler's room, in the Brigade Commander's suite. The gentleman Brigade Commander agreed and with that lost his stripes the week before the game.

January 1, 1959 marked final victory for Fidel Castro's revolution in Cuba. It was more than a vignette for *Godfather II*. His predecessor had been a hated, mobbed-up dictator. For a short time Castro's victory was welcomed stateside. Castro's economic plans and global alliances were murky, at least for a brief time. But eventually they became clear and thus a matter that would occupy the nation and the USNA class of '60 for years to come.

A month later, according to Don McLean, "the music died."

In another part of the music world back in the late 1950s there was a pleasant-voiced, white male recording star, Pat Boone, who was trying to become the next Bing Crosby. He was also trying to position himself to the goody-two-shoes side of Elvis Presley. But it was a fact, of which he seemed oblivious, that music had moved on. When he recorded a mildly up-tempo cover version of Little Richard's 1955 high-energy *Tutti-frutti*—a version that even rose higher on the charts than the super-energetic black performer's—disk jockeys finally rebelled and brought black music, as performed by black vocalists, into the mainstream. Still, in the spring of 1959 he had a weekly TV show probably mostly appealing to anti-rock-and-roll, Lawrence-Welk loving, "traditionalists."

At that point he came to do a show at the Naval Academy during the week leading up to 1960's Ring Dance. It did not go well. Remember, this was before videotape. A planned audience participation number of him singing "Deep in the Heart of Texas" (Clap, Clap, Clap) in the mess hall went raucous to the point of bordering on a food fight. Times were changing. The kindest published review of the show called it "appalling."

During those years the Navy had been trying to figure out how it was going to get its piece of the nuclear arms race. To that end it had designed and built a jet seaplane, the P6M. It was being built at the Martin Aircraft factory near Baltimore and was being tested over Chesapeake Bay. The first two had fatal in-flight failures involving the tail control surfaces going haywire. It was scrapped but by then a new idea, the Polaris missile, had come along. (In 1960, the first one displayed on campus was instantly paint-camouflaged as a Coke bottle.)

The football season of '60's 1/C year included a game against the University of Maryland, the "Terrapins." That rivalry, unlike the mutually respectful one with Army, was more akin to the genuinely enmity-filled one between Michigan and Ohio State. The Brigade fully expected a riot (a riot it would not start) after the game. Many Mids came with bank-paper-wrapped rolls of coins in their overcoat pockets should their fists need a bit more oomph. The riot became more likely with the frustration for Maryland when time ran out for its team as it was driving for a winning touchdown on Navy's 2-yard line. Mids gathered on the field to meet their dates but somehow the twerps among the Terps decided it would be nice to run among them and swipe a cap for a souvenir. Many little battles followed from that.

Jack - One sticks in my mind. The donnybrook seemed to be all over and I was climbing the stairs toward the exit, though looking over my shoulder at the few skirmishes still in progress. One Terp came running up the next aisle over carrying a cap. There was a streak of blue on my right that went between the seats to that aisle in a flash and hit the Terp-perp with a tackle that would have made Ronnie Lott proud. The Terp went sprawling into the seats beyond and the blue streak returned the cap to its owner. I knew him just a bit. As I write this, about a year and a half back, our class president sent us his obit written by his widow, the once-young Brazilian lady whom I had met long ago on the way to view a sunset in Rio.

Later that fall of 1959, on the day after Saturday's Army-Navy football game, a TV trivia show forerunner of *Jeopardy*, *The GE College Bowl*, held an Army-Navy contest of its own. Navy trotted out its stars, including an NCAA champion Olympics-bound fencer from the class of '60 who had studied Russian and had just attended a White House dinner honoring the visiting Chairman Khrushchev. All three on the Navy panel of contestants were selected to best show the accomplishments of USNA's students during the mid-show interview and still win. And they did. (But, respect for USMA requires truth be told: it was very competitive, off camera before the live show, our brothers on the Hudson had won 2 of the 3 rehearsal games.) Sixty years later a plebe in the class of 2020 competed in the 15-school Jeopardy College Tournament, made the finals, and finished second.

As 1959 turned into 1960 and graduation approached, '60's role of being on the cusp of change was still in force. The class was the last class in which service and ship selection was done in an order set by a lottery—it being the belief that too much of one's career was already subject to class standing. Also, 1960 became the first class able to go directly to submarine service; earlier classes had to go to sea for a year before sub school. There were 50 such slots open to members of the class. The next class, '61, was the first to be allowed direct entry into Nuclear Power School. The last change affecting the class's short term future was that 1960 became the first class that was not afforded 60 days leave at graduation. Actually this wasn't as harsh as it seems; the second 30 days had been granted as an advance on the assumption that, as a practical matter, during a new graduate's first year of sea duty, his commanding officer would not allow any of the 30 days leave he would accrue in his first year. *Jack—But the fleet was relaxing. I was able to take 10 days that year (out of a total of 30 days over the 4 years during which I had shipboard responsibilities).*

Through it all the class of 1960 was shrinking. Of the 1080 counted in its ranks 797, 73.8%, graduated.

With summer school make-ups and more limited roll-backs the class of 2020 had about half as much attrition. 1013 of its starting 1183, 85.6%, made it to graduation.

As those remaining in 2020 came back from their final Christmas Leave ready to tear into one more semester on the road to freedom, events were developing in a town in China they, and the rest of us, had never heard about.

With the next leave period being spring break, the dark ages[1] loomed as the final challenge for the class of '20. The service assignments were decided before Thanksgiving. Those selections now seemed more real as the service uniforms began arriving and were worn on "Warrior Wednesdays." 1/2" stripes were sewn on new Service Dress Blue jackets, and plans were more or less solidified for families heading to Annapolis in May. These events were standard for this time of year as the graduating class approached, at long last, the end of their four years by the Severn.

Two nights before the end of the dark ages, marked by the beginning of spring break leave, the Brigade assembled to hear a message from the Commandant of Midshipmen and the Chief of Medicine. The assembly was held to discuss the recent news of an outbreak of COVID-19 in China, and as far as midshipmen were concerned, this public panic was good joke fodder and nothing else. The Commandant's message was essentially a request to be smart, stay safe, and above all, "Stay away from clubs!" The joke went down in history on anonymous USNA social media meme pages.

Of course, history as it rolled out told us this joke was emerging as a global pandemic resulting in the loss of hundreds of thousands of lives. Like students at every other college in the United States, Midshipmen were delayed in their return

---

1. "The Dark Ages" is the century-old term for the drear days in the new year when Mids go to class with the North wind blowing sleet in their right ears and return from class giving their left ears equal opportunity for misery.

Chapter 21 - Wrapping Up

from spring break, first by two weeks. That delay lasted for the remainder of the year. Any concept of the graduation that the Academy had ever known became a fading hope as the staff and leadership on the Yard scrambled to find solutions to the unending list of problems that COVID presented.

When the Administration formally announced the cancellation of the traditional graduation, our contributor, Spencer, something of a class chronicler, posted her initial reaction, including gratitude to alums who expressed empathetic sorrow for 2020's apparent loss. And she noted "As a group of people who have worked over the past four years to show strength in adversity, letting ourselves feel this disappointment is not easy." In it she expressed a longing for the apparently lost communion of the celebratory ritual tossing of caps to the sky.

Later she wrote an opinion piece on the subject that is well worth reading for a more extensive and sensitive understanding of the effect of that initial announcement on members of the class of 2020 than we can give here. It was published, with her picture, in the Capital Gazette, "To my Naval Academy classmates, we will feel this forever." You can read it at tiny.cc/ca21-1 (or scan QR21-1 on page 159).

With all of this in mind, we must note that the rest of the United States was not in any better shape. With the economy crashing, many millions out of work, businesses shut, supply chains halted, and COVID fatalities rising rapidly, the loss of '20's graduation ceremony paled; and '20 knew it.

While we'll tell of the solutions that leadership at USNA eventually arrived at, that will do no justice to the amount of work put in for all of the solutions that were worked over but eventually discarded.

At first, communication to Midshipmen was slow and unsatisfactory, and uncertainty loomed. Academics shifted, as best USNA was able, to online classes taught through video chat rooms. Initially there was little consistency among instructors on which chat rooms to use for class, how homework was to be submitted, and how attendance to class should be tracked. But eventually the turmoil subsided. Even some extra-curricular activities resumed, witness the Glee Club's effort at tiny.cc/ca21-2 (or scan QR21-2 on page 159).

Military training for the plebes became almost non-existent. While they were held accountable for their academic performance, all training events including the traditional Herndon Climb and professional competency boards were postponed until further notice. "Sea Trials" (a one-day, end of year, exhausting physical fitness challenge) was conducted virtually, with plebes completing physical events from their remote locations.

May arrived with the Air Force Academy having already graduated its cadets. USNA decided to bring back the class of '20 in five waves for out-processing and an amended ceremony. Each wave of about 200 1/C received one day to move out of

Bancroft and cycle through various stations to receive their diplomas, collect their medical records, return swords, rifles, and confidential publications, and sign their Oaths of Office. The following day centered about a socially-distanced graduation ceremony in Tecumseh Court for each 200-person cohort, the first and hopefully only of its kind to ever take place. The fifth wave was favored with three fly-overs by the Blue Angels. On May 22nd, 2020 the Academy streamed a virtual ceremony containing footage of the five separate ceremonies in T-Court and recorded speeches from USNA leadership, the Chief of Naval Operations, and the Secretary of Defense.

While this was not the graduation ceremony that anyone had envisioned for 2020, the efforts by the Administration, faculty, and staff to give 2020 the same honor as every class before it was sincere and welcomed. The collective feeling among the class of 2020 is one of appreciation for the efforts of all, and stoic recognition of the fact that the world was changing and this was but one small piece of the global effects of the pandemic. While the feeling of disappointment was inescapable, it was not overwhelming.

The joy, the triumph, of having "made it" still propelled caps into the air with enthusiasm at least the equal of any class in the last 64 years.

Very respectfully,
    Josh, Spencer, Rick, Rob, and Jack

Chapter 21 - Wrapping Up

QR21-1

tiny.cc/ca21-1

QR21-2

tiny.cc/ca21-2

EPILOGUE

NOT ONLY DID 2020 MISS THE TRADITIONAL COMMISSIONING WEEK but summer training came to a sudden and unexpected halt, Plebe Summer was in jeopardy, and there was no certainty that the Brigade would be able to return for the next academic term. The Administration had to come up with compromises that supported both the safety of the Midshipmen and staff as well as the readiness requirements of the Navy and Marine Corps.

To its well-deserved credit, the current Administration has measured up to demands for managerial agility few would have expected it to face. Whether, ultimately, the choices it makes will spare the school from the contagion only time will tell. But, from the perspective of an informed old grad and four new grads working on plebe summer assignments while awaiting their classes at specific Navy-community schools, the Administration has made intelligent, informed choices and implemented those decisions with the speed and firmness the circumstances demand.

For example, when the new mids, plebes of the class of 2024, arrived for their plebe summer they had already been asked to self-quarantine for 2 weeks. And then, upon arrival, they were quarantined for two weeks more. That excepted, plebe summer ran its course—unwelcome to the plebes but satisfactorily as judged by three of us who participated.

Then in mid-August, as the Brigade re-formed, some of the returning upperclass, but less than 2%, tested COVID positive. To achieve social distancing, for the first time in its history, Bancroft did not house the entire Brigade. The neighboring St. John's College[1] having closed for the fall semester, offered use of its facilities to the Academy and 397 Mids from the 4th Battalion moved to quarters in its dormitories, equipped by the Navy to support remote instruction.

In mid-September, 2020 *U. S. News & World Report* published its annual college rankings. USNA is still 1st among public colleges but it is no longer 17th among liberal arts colleges; it is in a 3-way tie for 6th.

Most recently, the federal case to block the expulsion of the racist Mid was settled on undisclosed terms while it was on an interim appeal following a series of bizarre rulings by a District Court Judge who apparently wanted to mother the poor boy.

But all that, and that which will happen between our writing and your reading (and beyond) is proper copy for someone else's book.

---

1. The nation's third oldest college and about as different from USNA as possible—ultra-modern in the sense that it was seen as hippie-central in '60's day before there were hippies; yet ultra-traditional in the sense of its "Great Books" study-of-the classics curriculum.

APPENDIX A

THE NIGHTCRAWLERS[1]

The Cast:

    Class of '60
        Dick Burgess (19th Co)
        Bob Bengston (19th Co)
        George (Rusty) Dowell (19th Co)
        Norman (Mouse) Jones (19th Co)
        Sam McKee (16th Co)
        Bob (Moke) Meck (19th Co)
        Dan Reid (19th Co)
        Don Weatherson (19th Co)

    Class of '62
        Joe Roberts (19th Co)

The Time: Late April 1959
The Place: Worden Field, USNA
The Idea: During exchange weekend at West Point, some of us roomed with

---

1. Courtesy of Bob Meck.

some WooPoos who were members of the Mole Society. This motley group took advantage of the steam-heating tunnels, which connected the buildings on the Plain at the Point, by executing a variety of pranks and dirty tricks in the Sup's office and the various classrooms. Upon returning to the Yard at USNA, we decided to plan something analogous to Mole Society pranks. It being spring set P-rade time, we decided to make these monotonous Wednesday afternoons interesting.

The Plan: We chose to rearrange the guidon blocks on Worden Field so that during the march-on phase of the parade, two companies from each regiment would find themselves with no place to form in the normal line of troops. We chose the specific Wednesday for the dirty deed and engaged in final planning. Two teams of four (all from '60) would work together to dig up the guidon blocks and dispose of them in College Creek. After disposing of four blocks, each team (one per regiment) would redistribute the remaining blocks evenly along the line of troops, so that there would be no noticeable gap between companies. The class of '62 participant would serve as lookout for Jimmy Legs.[2] The operation would commence at midnight, and the uniform would be working dress blue shirts and dungaree trousers.

The Operation: At the appointed time, we departed Mother Bancroft via the band room in the basement of the fourth wing, sprinted tactically and reassembled at the bandstand at Worden Field. Armed with bayonets for our "yard work" we moved out to our "regimental duty stations." Jimmy Leg patrols slowed us twice, but in about an hour's time, we had dug up four blocks, ditched them in the creek, and rearranged the other twenty. Then we returned via the band room to our rooms and awaited the afternoon parade.

The Parade: For the first time since plebe summer, there were at least nine Mids who looked forward to the parade. At noon meal, a plebe announced that the reviewing officials for the parade would be the senior flag officers of each of NATO's Navies. Well, they were in for the treat of their lives. The regiments formed and off we all marched to Worden. What began as a sharp and orderly left turn and march to the company right guide blocks became a serpentine movement as the last battalions tried to form ranks. Finally, the 11th and 12th Companies and the 23rd and 24th Companies found themselves "blockless." Being those quick thinking leaders of '59, the company commanders formed their companies behind the 1st and 2nd and 13th and 14th companies. When the command "Pass In Review" was sounded and companies paid their "eyes right" respect to the reviewing officials, one could easily

---

2. Civilian uniformed police that guarded the gates and performed various security duties around the campus.

spot the bright red and purple bulging blood vessels around the Supe's Service Dress White collar. We would be toast were we to be identified as the culprits.

The Aftermath: After some days, we decided to rub some salt in the wounds of the oppressed Class of '59 leadership. Dan Reid wrote a stirring letter to Salty Sam (the gossip columnist in the campus magazine, *The Log*, which applauded the coolness under fire exhibited by the indomitable First Class. The letter was signed "NIGHTCRAWLERS." Some weeks passed and on one fateful Saturday morning before noon meal formation, Lieutenant Thompson (19th Company Officer) summoned us into his office and asked if by any chance we were members of the Nightcrawlers. We acknowledged the fact, and after noon formation, were escorted to the Commandant's office, where we were chastised, given our Class As, and directed to write letters of apology to each of the Flags who had reviewed the parade. Restrictions lasted until graduation day, but we were given a two-hour reprieve to attend the ring dance (dip the ring, kiss our OAO, dance one dance and head back to the Battalion Office for muster). Finally, it was great being free after graduation to begin our First Class cruise and think back on that memorable P-Rade in late April.

APPENDIX B

The True Story of the Virgin Cannons
By Glenn Coleman, Jim McKinney, Dave Parkinson (11)[1]

This factual story is set forth with confidence that the statute of limitations for the potential Class A and its 75 and 30 has expired.

On a cold and rainy afternoon in April, 1959 the three of us were sitting around our room in the doldrums. We needed some action. We had a stash of cherry bombs given to us by an Academy Professor who shall remain anonymous. We looked at an alarm clock on the desk and a light went off. How about activating the Virgin Cannons?

Over the next several days we concocted a plan—rig up a cherry time bomb set to go off at Saturday noon formation and put it in a Virgin Canon. Simply put, an alarm clock minus the minute hand would be wired to complete an electrical circuit at about 12:05 p.m. The circuit would consist of a flash bulb, a battery, and the clock. Secured to the flash bulb with some airplane dope were some matches and the fuses to two cherry bombs. We tested the gimmick several times, minus the cherry bombs, of course, and were confident the crude device would work. But the time of detonation could only be guessed at within +/- 5 minutes of the appointed time.

We decided on Saturday noon meal formation on April 29, 1959. The weather was supposed to be good, and there would be a large crowd gathered for the formation and the ensuing liberty. There was only one issue left—how to get the device into

---
1. Courtesy of Jim McKinney.

one of the cannons unseen. The circuit was only good for 12 hours, so it had to be put in the cannon after Friday midnight. Glenn Coleman was on the excused squad with a bad knee, so Jim McKinney and Dave Parkinson became the designated muzzleloaders. We set our alarm clocks and got up at 1 a.m. and set the timing device. Under cover of darkness we sneaked out of the 5th Wing, around the 1st Wing, to the left Virgin Cannon (facing Bancroft Hall). Jim climbed on Dave's shoulders and was hoisted up to the muzzle. In went the timing device, along with an ample charge of talcum powder to simulate a smoke blast. We quickly returned to the 5th Wing, were let in the door by Glenn, and went to our room without being detected by an Officer of the Watch (OOW), Midshipman Officer of the Watch (MOOW), or a CMA.[2] Needless to say, a sleepless night ensued.

All went as planned. The first detonation occurred just as the Brigade Staff halted after countermarching between the cannons! The first cherry bomb detonated in a cloud of talcum powder, and the force of the explosion blew the second cherry bomb towards the second cannon where it detonated.

Much discussion immediately ensued, and speculation had already started running rampant about who the perpetrators may have been. As we headed out from Bancroft Hall after the noon meal formation, we noticed a crowd gathering around the CMA and Jimmy Legs, who had just retrieved what was left of the clock from the cannon muzzle. When Jim came up and asked the Jimmy Legs what he had, he responded, "Evidence" with an outstretched hand. Within a wink, Jim snatched the remnants of the clock out of his hands to look at it, and passed it around. With that any fingerprint evidence was duly compromised.

Rejoining the throngs of midshipmen headed out for afternoon liberty, we hit on a campaign to defocus any internal investigation. Since the University of Maryland was playing Navy in Lacrosse that day, we started a rumor that these bitter rivals must have been responsible for the prank.

Adm. Charley Melson and his staff were becoming perturbed at the antics of another group, the Night Crawlers (moving airplanes, rearranging Parade Field guide blocks). They called in the Office of Naval Intelligence—specifically its sub-branch, the Naval Investigative Service[3]—to investigate the pranks. Probably relieved to have an assignment other than following sailors into airport restrooms, that branch proceeded with vigor.

As to the virgin cannon caper it deduced that some residual material from fabrication or testing must still exist within Bancroft. When unannounced room

---

2. "Chief Master at Arms" who comprised part of the combined Midshipmen/Officer watch team.

3. Later, in 1966, to be spun out of ONI as NCIS and go on even later to be romanticized in 3 separate TV series.

searches throughout Bancroft (while room occupants were at class) turned up nothing, ONI concluded the indicting residual material must be locked away in some first or second classman's confidential publications safe. So they started on a rampage of room-to-room searches of the safes.

In fact, Dave and Jim did still have some residuals (cherry bombs/flash bulbs/wires) in their safes. But ONI's safe-search exercise could not be conducted in a clandestine manner as each searched Mid had to use his private combination to open his safe. Word reached us and we decided to put all the evidence in our steam kits [4] and take the kits along, as usual, on our next YP training. There we dumped the stuff off the YP's fantail into the Chesapeake. We were feeling very smug about it until we looked up at the pilot deck and saw the YP's salty chief looking down on us in a puzzled manner. Our fears were allayed when he gestured with a zippering motion over his mouth to reassure us, "They're not going to hear it from me."

---

4. *Jack - normally holding mechanical drawing and navigation implements like dividers, compasses, parallel rules, etc.*

Made in the USA
Middletown, DE
22 January 2022